WOMAN

AN ASSET TO THE NATION

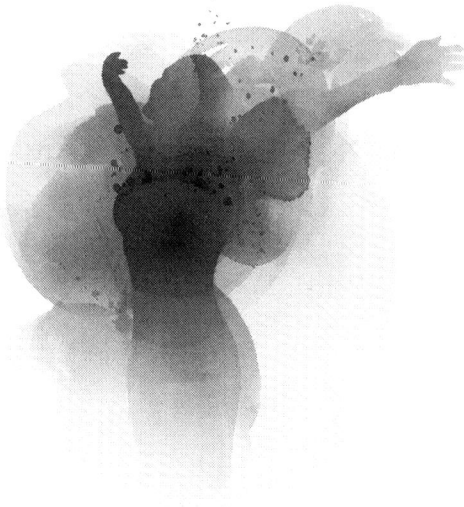

NIKE ADEYEMI

Printed in the United States of America

ACKNOWLEDGEMENTS

I express my appreciation to the amazing people who made this book a reality. The staff at Pneuma Publishing for proofreading and editing the original manuscript. GodKulture for editing this edition and designing the page layout. My family, friends, mentors, protégés and associates who encourage and support me.

I appreciate my sweetheart, Sam. Growing together has brought opportunities to make the world a better place. I am grateful for our children Sophie, David and Adora for their understanding and love.

I am most grateful to God for grace and love beyond measure.

CONTENTS

PREFACE

W omen are not an accident that has already happened or that are about to happen. A woman is neither evil much less a necessary evil. The truth is that women are the masterpiece of God's creation and have their place in God's scheme of things on the earth and for all humanity.

One must concede, though, that women are very complex beings, requiring high-grade thinking to understand and appreciate. But this is not a minus. In fact, our complexity is part of God's infinite wisdom in His creation plan. We agree that a misunderstanding exists about the true identity of 'the woman'. Most men are confused about who a woman truly is. Amazingly, many women know no better. They don't know why 'the woman' is what she is.

As a woman, I am appalled by the amount of false information being peddled about in various homes and the society at large concerning the nature of women. It is true that W-O-M-A-N is What-Our-Men-Are-Not. It is however not true that she is irrelevant in what is falsely called a man's world or some disposable burden.

This book is meant to lift up women on the high stage of relevance and demonstrate their potential. You need to know that the female carries the womb that births the whole human race. You also need to know that the peculiar natural qualities of women are to better the lot of the man. Her smile brightens the world, just as her quick tears wet and soften the hard hearts of men.

Even her "too much talking" is a signal to her potential to 'ring the tones' of heaven and move the hand of Almighty God through her supplications. What else can be more needed today than praying women as we see the escalating incidences of the abuse of women across the world!

The few who have discovered the true concept about being a woman celebrate her. And none has done so better than God who made her. Do you wonder that the Bible is replete with astonishing exultation of womanhood? I plead with all readers, men and women alike, to see *Woman, An Asset To The Nations* as a reflection of the biblical woman - The Real Woman. The holy writ helps us to see into God's inner thoughts for creating this gender, and enables us to appreciate the true beauty and role of this masterpiece we call WOMAN.

When you have had this understanding, take action with a change of heart towards women and meet me at the confident and fulfilled side of life.

Nike Adeyemi

CHAPTER 1

ESSENCE
OF
WOMANHOOD

L et me begin this discourse by reviewing 1 Samuel 9:10-14, a text that offers much for us to glean about the essence of womanhood.

"Then Saul said to his servant, "Well said; come, let us go." So they went to the city where the man of God was. As they went up the hill to the city, they met some young women going out to draw water, and said to them, "Is the seer here?" And they answered them and said, "Yes, there he is, just ahead of you. Hurry now; for today he came to this city, because there is a sacrifice of the people today on the high place. As soon as you come into the city, you will surely find him before he goes up to

WOMAN

the high place to eat. For the people will not eat until he comes, because he must bless the sacrifice; afterward those who are invited will eat. Now therefore, go up, for about this time you will find him." So they went up to the city. As they were coming into the city, there was Samuel, coming out toward them on his way up to the high place."

The Bible is full of symbolism that shows women as embodiments of hidden treasures to be discovered, dug out, diligently mined, affectionately nurtured, and cautiously coddled to bring out their gracious fragrance.

"Surely there is a mine for silver, and a place where gold is refined. Iron is taken from the earth, And copper is smelted from ore."[1]

Consider the value of gold, which is what Job is talking about here. Gold is not cheap, nor is womanhood cheap. Gold is not found on the surface of the earth or just anywhere. Anyone looking for gold must dig for it.

One thing we know about gold is that it does not remain where it is mined. It is dug out and processed to be used as ornaments or as gifts. Gold is mined from the earth but ends up beautifying people's bodies and homes. Similarly, a woman is to see herself from that perspective. Let us continue to unveil the value God has placed on women.

Your position before God

There is a place God picked you from, and there is a place He has reserved for you. As women, we must discover why God created us the way we are- generally and specifically as individuals. You need to ask the Lord, "Where is my place?" You see, God has ordained women to make a difference on the earth.

Recall that, when God made the man in the beginning, man went about his business. But God thought that life could be better, the earth could be better, man could be better and produce more with the woman. This must be why God made the woman. Each time I remember this, I like to say, "O God, thank You for making me a woman."

God did not have to make us. We did not have to exist. The fact that He created us points to the important role He intends us to play in the world. After He made the woman, God took her to the man and said, "Take."[2] This is why every woman should see herself as an embodiment of a gift to her husband. You were given to your man's purposes, to his work, to everything that would come out of him. Beyond your man, you were also given to bless the whole earth.

As a woman, I used to wonder why the woman's life is perpetually on the giving end, especially as a wife and mother. Even spinsters live by giving! When the chips are down, people tend to turn to women for help. It appears unfair. The woman gives to her husband and children, to relatives and the society at large, and sometimes, nobody remembers her. I have since learned, however, that it's all God's design. The sooner this sinks in and we begin to accept this innate role as women, the better.

Stop murmuring!

I have since stopped complaining and whining about the position of the man over his wife, because I have discovered that this is how God made us. It may look unfair, but it is fair to the discerning woman who, seeing things from the perspective of God, understands that it is more blessed to give than to receive. As a woman, your second name is 'Gift', and as a gift - because God wanted to give through you - everything about you should revolve around giving. So, rather than go about looking for someone to bless us, we ought to look for someone to bless.

God made the woman unique. He filled her with compassion. As women, we must be careful, however, not to direct our compassion inwardly to the point of self-pity, which rightly described, is perverted compassion. When we complain about certain situations and whine over our seemingly helpless state, we demonstrate compassion, but are unwittingly turning it inwards.

A man and his wife make love, and it is the woman who becomes pregnant, and carries the burden of the unborn child for whole nine months. Yes, it looks unfair. But women, that's what God made you for. It's wrong to think that you came to this earth as a beast of burden. No. We are on earth to make a difference, to show love and compassion and make a positive impact. And we need not wait for anyone before we can make an impact. We are to allow God to process us from our raw state, to refine us from raw gold into ornaments, so we can beautify the lives of people and the community. We are to beautify our cities and nations. I pray that God will help you to discover your true value and place in Jesus' name.

Little glamour, Big difference

For the Christian woman, there is even a special role. We are *gates* and *entry points* through which people can find their way to heaven. God forbid that anyone should go to hell through their contact with me. But, you see, it has to be one of the two. No one should come in contact with you and remain the same. Our business is to make a difference on the earth. It does not have to be in a big and glamorous way, but in the little things we do in our careers, offices and at home. Just by changing diapers and loving that child, you are imparting something to the world. But you have to remember that, with most of these seemingly small acts of service, the results are long term.

Great men and women of God, and many others in the world, were nurtured from the cradle by the hands of some diligent woman. You do not have to preach or speak in a large arena to impact the world; we impact the world through everything we say and do with our tongue and our lifestyle. It is our responsibility to lift up the discouraged and make a significant difference in their lives. This is why we need to ask ourselves, "What am I imparting? Am I imparting life or death, or do I merely exist, imparting neither blessing nor a curse?" God has not called us to be idle, because, as Amos 6:1 says, "Woe to you who are at ease in Zion." We must be about, doing something for God, and being a blessing to humanity.

As a gate, you are an entry point through which people transmute into better human beings for God and for the society. Talking about an immoral woman in Proverbs 7:27, the Bible says, "Her house is the way to hell, descending to the chambers of death." But we are not to be gates to hell. The Christian woman is a gate to heaven. We are custodians of blessings. In Ecclesiastes.7:26, Solomon says, "And I find more bitter than death the woman whose heart is snares and nets, whose hands are fetters. He who pleases God shall escape from her, but the sinner shall be trapped by her." This is terrible!

Learning from experience

Solomon knew women well; he had a thousand of them: seven hundred wives and three hundred concubines. So he knew women of every shade and description intimately. In Ecclesiastes 7:26 Solomon said he found something "more bitter than death - the woman whose heart is snares and nets, whose hands are fetters." With her "snares and nets" and hands like "fetters", this woman traps and kills the men who are lured by her. The man that pleases God, Solomon concluded, shall escape her trap, but the sinner shall fall for her.

In case anyone should mistake this particular woman as a general archetype for all women, God, the originator of the idea of a woman, says no. All through Scriptures, there are positive things written about women, granted though that some negative things are said about women too. The negative things about women grieve my heart because right before our eyes in this day and age, we see women getting involved in all kinds of evil. But God is saying all that must change. As Christian women, we must be known for the ideals of womanhood. Because of us, when people think of women and womanhood, they should bless God for His foreknowledge and perfect creation.

No one should think of the woman as a necessary evil. God forbid! God has ordained us to be a blessing on earth. A societal change of attitude towards women has to start from our own hearts as women. We must open up to God and allow Him do His holy work in our lives. He wants to flow and express Himself to mankind through us. We should be willing to open up to God.

There were many women in Bible days as in contemporary time who have blessed womanhood and the world. Deborah, Jael and Esther, for instance, are among women of honor in the Bible. Even in our present day, we remember women - some dead and others still living - who have blessed the world with their lives. I pray that after you are gone, your memory in the lives of people would bring joy and greatness in Jesus' name.

A Host of Negative Women

From the beginning of time, there have always been women who have literally failed God; women like Herodias, the wife of King Herod, whom he married by fraud. She had been the wife of Philip, Herod's brother, but eloped with Herod. Her daughter had pleased the king when she danced at his birthday party. Herod then offered her a blank check, by saying, "You impressed me. Ask me anything and I would give you, up to half of my kingdom." That, you can see, was a reckless promise! Not knowing what to ask for, the naïve girl went to her mother to seek her advice; and the mother who had been nursing a grudge against John the Baptist because he disapproved of her marriage to Herod promptly seized on her moment of revenge: "Ask for the head of John the Baptist," she said. What a failure!

Herodias could have asked for better things, things that would better the lives of people. We are custodians of life. As a woman, whether you already have physical children or not, see yourself as a mother. See yourself as responsible for whoever interacts with you. See yourself as impacting their lives. This is a gracious and rewarding task, because it pleases God.

There was another woman called Michal, whom David married. She was the daughter of Saul, the first king of Israel. Her fault was ingratitude. She may be excused, though, because her life had been full of bitterness. She was raised by a father who turned his back against God. In her disillusion, she perhaps could not be expected to love her husband nor bless him even when he danced before God in praise and worship after God brought back the ark of covenant to Israel. Rather than join in the worship of God, Michal despised

King David, her husband, for what she felt was an unwarranted public display of emotion towards God. Her words full of sarcasm, she said to her husband, "How glorious was the king of Israel to day, who uncovered himself to day in the eyes of the handmaids of his servants, as one of the vain fellows shamelessly uncovereth himself!"[3]

She was basically saying, "Are you not a king? Why are you embarrassing yourself?" By her wrong attitude, she displeased God, and was punished with perpetual barrenness. I have mentioned this so we can decide what kind of women we want to be. We have a choice to deliberately open up to God to enable us be a blessing to all.

Second Chance from God

There was a woman called Rahab. She had been a perpetrator of evil as she was a harlot. But the Lord touched her heart; she was changed and was greatly used by the Lord. She opened up her home to the people of God and helped them when they were in need. For her kind deed, her life, with those of her entire household, was spared and delivered from the sudden destruction that befell the whole city of Jericho. This affirms that God is a God of second chances.

It does not matter how bad one has been. It does not matter what evil one has been into. It does not matter what manner of things one has done or said in the past. There is hope for anyone who accepts God's offer of salvation through Jesus Christ. Only Jesus can transform your life and make you live the way you ought.

I have written this book to bring all women to the place of conversion and influence, so God can empower and release His anointing upon us, which in turn will enable us go out there and be what we ought to be.

Will You Be Missed When You Die?

You may have read the story of Dorcas; she was another godly woman. Her life blesses and inspires me each time I read about her. Acts 9:36 says, "At Joppa there was a certain disciple named Tabitha, which is translated Dorcas. This woman was full of good works and charitable deeds which she did."

What follows in the story reveals that she fell ill and later died. The news of her death moved so many hearts. Widows and the entire community cried and wailed for Dorcas. There are people you miss greatly when they die. There are others whose death brings relief of some sort; you just do not miss them. One of the leaders in Nigeria got exactly that response in 1998. Ordinarily, the death of a leader should cause grief across the whole nation. The people should mourn. But in his case there was jubilation across the land.

It was a case of good riddance. The people rejoiced at his death. In Dorcas' case, the widows in particular, were inconsolable. To them, Dorcas had been such a blessing. "See the coat she made for me; she blessed my life," those women testified of her. The Bible says, in verse 39, that Apostle Peter was called into the upper room where Dorcas was laid, with "all the widows [standing] by him weeping, showing the tunics and garments which Dorcas had made while she was with them." Peter then asked the wailing women to step out of the room so he could be alone to pray. He prayed and Dorcas came back to life and then he presented her alive to the people. May God continually present you alive! A woman of worth is usually regarded too relevant to the earth to be taken away before her time.

I have the feeling that God loved Dorcas just as much as He did Enoch. The Bible says Enoch walked with God and God just took him away. It's almost like He said, "You're just too good for the earth, come and join Me up here in heaven. Let's continue our fellowship up here" God took Dorcas away too. But constrained by the wailing and cries of those women, God had to release Dorcas to continue her good works to humanity. God seemed to say, "I can't stand the grief that these people are expressing." The life of Dorcas is one we should all emulate.

Going Beyond the Pulpit

It is in taking our place as women that we become relevant, not by competing with men. This is how our cities and nations, indeed the whole earth, can be healed. When we take our place in bringing up our children aright, they won't grow up into armed robbers. A woman may not have a pulpit as a platform for preaching - Dorcas had none, yet she was a blessing to her community. Our cities are waiting for us. Wherever you find yourself as a woman, see yourself as an angel planted there by the Lord. We undermine our capacity when we fail to see the hand of God in what we do and where He leads us per time. God has a superior motive for your being where you are, and you need to tap into His purpose and help Him to fulfill His agenda on the earth. Dorcas took her place. You can take yours too.

God Manifests Power in Obscurity

Psalm 68:11 tells us that "The Lord gave the word; Great was the company of those who proclaimed it." Reading the original translation of this text, I discovered that God was talking about women. Some translations actually read, "...great was the company of women that told it." *Great are the company of women set and arrayed for warfare.* And that was the word the Lord ministered to me when He began to speak to me about the Real Woman initiative. He said, "Go out there and raise for Me a special breed of women who would make a difference in the world and would birth My purposes and be a blessing." As I look around, I see that the company is still very few in number. God spoke of a great, large and massive company of women set for Him. I believe that God's company of women is growing day by day.

Verse 12 of this psalm adds: "Kings of armies flee, they flee, And she who remains at home divides the spoil." I read this verse with so much amusement. The Holy Spirit is actually saying that she who takes and stays in her place will divide the spoil. That reminds me of Jael.

Jael was relatively unknown in the book of Judges. We know of Deborah in her public ministry. Jael, the wife of Abner the Canaanite, had no such public ministry. She was at home in her tent. She may have come to the point when she said, "Lord, when will I be released from washing pots and pans? When will I be

WOMAN

released from baby care and such stuff? I want to do more for You. I believe there is more to life than just being in the kitchen." Her day of opportunity eventually came. Jael's ministry was hospitality. She knew this, and stayed there. Hers wasn't about taking up a weapon and going to war or in our day, the microphone to preach at crusades or in church. Through her hospitality, she defeated Sisera, the enemy of her nation.

Sisera had fled the battle against Israel. As he fled past the house of Jael, he sought temporary shelter because he took Abner for his friend. But God had designed it so. Jael, who was home, invited the fleeing warrior in. He came in believing he was in safe hands. He wanted water, but she generously offered him milk instead. Some gracious women are like that. You visit them casually, but they go into the kitchen and cook for you the best of meals, because that's their area of impact.

Sisera felt cool, as Jael made him sleep - feeling really safe. But at the end of the story, we see Jael take a nail which she drove into the temple of the weary warrior. When the soldiers of Israel who were all about looking for Sisera came around, she simply called them in to see the enemy of the nation dead at her feet. God wants to give us such sweat-less victories as we stay in our place.

The psalm continues in verse 13, "Though you lie down among the sheepfolds, You will be like the wings of a dove covered with silver, And her feathers with yellow gold." This refers to the place where animals, whether sheep or cows are kept and fed with water and grass. In Bible days, that was the assignment for women. They went to draw water for the sheep. Likewise, I say to you, "Though you have stayed among the sheepfold, you will be like the wings of the dove covered with silver, and your feathers with yellow gold." That talks about prosperity, you know. It goes to show that your prosperity is in the place of your assignment.

Stay Where God Has Placed You

Woman, God has ordained it that you have your own substance. In Luke 8, the Bible talks about some women who followed Jesus and ministered to Him from their own substance. The substance was not the money their husbands gave them for housekeeping. Using housekeeping money for other things without your husband's approval would be wrong. These women had personal money they could use at their own discretion. They had substance that was their own because they stayed in the place of their assignment.

Back now to our first text in 1Samuel 9:10-11. "Then Saul said to his servant, "Well said; come, let us go." So they went to the city where the man of God was." As they went up the hill to the city, they met some young women going out to draw water, and said to them, "Is the seer here?"

Drawing water from wells for domestic use was a common occupation for women in Palestine in those days. You may already know the case of the Samaritan woman who Jesus asked to give Him water in John 4. He ended up giving her the water of life and thereby transforming and making her a distributor of God's blessings and mercy.

In this case, these women went up the hill to draw water too. Saul met them as he sought his father's donkeys that were lost. At this time, Saul had not been ordained king over Israel. He and his servant had been everywhere searching for the missing animals. His utter loss compelled him to accede to his servant's suggestion that they seek the man of God somewhere around, who as a prophet and a seer, could tell them where to find the lost flock. They were on their way looking for the man of God when they met these women who gave them direction. The role of these women in the unfolding process of Saul becoming king later is now etched in the history of Israel. See, your opportunity will come in the place where God has put you.

Drawing Water, Showering Blessing

We read a similar story in Genesis when Abraham sent his chief servant to go in search of a wife for his son, Isaac. Genesis 24:10-11 says, "Then the servant took ten of his master's camels and departed, for all his master's goods were in his hand. And he arose and went to Mesopotamia, to the city of Nahor. And he made his camels kneel down outside the city by a well of water at evening time, the time when women go out to draw water."

You can see, here again, that drawing water for household use seemed to be a major occupation of women in those days. It was something they did generally. The servant of Abraham said in verses 12 and 13, "O LORD God of my master Abraham, please give me success this day, and show kindness to my master Abraham. Behold, here I stand by the well of water, and the daughters of the men of the city are coming out to draw water."

As I read that, I reflect on the nocturnal activities of certain women in our cities. They go out, not to "draw water," but go out to give their bodies to men in exchange for money. It's an 'evil under the sun', and I pray that God uproots this curse from our cities in Jesus' name. God wants every woman to go draw water and be a blessing to our households. Isaiah 12:3 says, "Therefore with joy you will draw water from the wells of salvation."

Jesus is the Well of Salvation, the Fountain of Life and Living Water. He is the Bread of Life; and anyone under the bondage of immorality can receive deliverance in the name of Jesus. He is the only one that can quench our thirst and give us the Water that satisfies.

Abraham's servant prayed that the young woman to whom he would say, "Please let down your pitcher that I may drink," and she says, "Drink, and I will also give your camels a drink" - let her be the one You have appointed for Your servant Isaac." When Rebekah showed up, before the words were out of his mouth, she willingly gave him enough to drink, gave his fellow servants and camels too. She went the extra mile. She used her hospitality beyond measure. She used the place where the Lord had put her to bless that man. Little did she know that her kind gesture would lead her to become the wife of a great man, and by that, fulfill the purpose of God. Isaac, we know, was a vital link in God's promise to the nation of Israel and ultimately the world. And, as the only wife of Isaac, Rebekah became the mother of Jacob and the great posterity of Israel.

Before Rebekah left home for her matrimony, her relatives blessed Rebekah and said to her: "Our sister, may you become The mother of thousands of ten thousands; And may your descendants possess The gates of those who hate them." These prophecies, you may already know, happened with time as pronounced; and that is what God wants to do through us as women. Jesus says, "Occupy till I come"[4]. He is saying, "Take your place till I come. Do business till I come; go out and draw water and be a blessing." There is a place God has ordained for you to be a blessing. It could be in your career or job. Stay in your place and keep excelling in your assignments. God will make you a tremendous blessing to the world.

Opening Up to God

The women who Saul and servant met on their way to seeking Prophet Samuel answered them in 1Samuel 9:12-13, "Yes, there he is, just ahead of you. Hurry now; for today he came to this city, because there is a sacrifice of the people today on the high place. As soon as you come into the city, you will surely find him before he goes up to the high place to eat. For the people will not eat until he comes, because he must bless the sacrifice; afterward those who are invited will eat. Now therefore, go up, for about this time you will find him."

Of course, Saul and his servant found Samuel who prophesied upon Saul. God had told the prophet about him. And forthwith, Saul was turned into another man, as God made him the captain or king of Israel.

Reading this story, we tend to overlook the role of the women. They were instrumental to the blessings that came on Saul. As women, our daily prayer as carriers of God's blessings should be to bless the people we meet each day. That is why we must work on ourselves. This is the foundation. We must allow God to heal and deliver us from certain things so He can use us. It's not that we will be perfect or completely whole before we can be a blessing, but we must be ready and open to be used of God.

All Saul asked those women was, "Is the seer here?" Beyond the simple answer required, the reply of the women took quite some verses. That's typical of us, you know. We are very verbal. God wants to use our loquacious skill positively, not in the negative talkativeness that invariably produces sin. A woman's capacity with the tongue is an asset if put to good use. Used in prayer and preaching the gospel, our tongue becomes a source of blessing. The tongue is an asset when it ceases to be a virtue to be silent. In Isaiah 62:1, for instance, the prophet says, "For Zion's sake I will not hold My peace, and for Jerusalem's sake I will not rest, until her righteousness goes forth as brightness, and her salvation as a lamp that burns."

So, you have license to talk and declare things; it only depends on what you are saying. When this revelation hit my spirit, I literally let loose, especially in my prayer closet. You need to talk and decree things and watch how your words change things. The women in our story let loose their tongue positively, and went on and on, giving Saul details, as it were, 'downloading' everything about the city; and that information really blessed Saul.

Where You Belong

The important question you may be asking now is how to know where to begin. How do you take your place and become relevant? From the encounter of Saul with those women, the Lord gave me six keys to finding your place.

1. Be Informed
You need to be informed about your environment to take your rightful place. Get to know your community and city well. You cannot afford to limit your knowledge to cooking condiments. You see, the reason, sometimes, why our husbands tune off and are unable to love and communicate with us as we wish, could be because we preoccupy them with talk about the prices of groceries mainly. For a man, that is a bore. Beyond domestic chores, you need to be informed. Read the papers. Know about your husband's area of work or profession to enable you both share a discussion in his interest areas.

When you do this, you may be surprised at your potential for absorbing and knowing much more than you previously thought. We have wombs for bearing babies, you know. Our minds are like wombs too. You have the capacity to be highly productive than you think. It's just that either people have suppressed you far too long, or you have suppressed yourself. But things are changing in many quarters these days. Even men are confirming it in the secular world that women have great potentials as do the men. God is lifting old barriers and traditional stereotypes. He is healing the female gender. Gender reconciliation is happening everywhere!

Already in the world of business and governments, decision makers are beginning to invite and involve women at top levels. The men have suddenly woken up to the realization that as mothers, we are wired up to carefully nurture and care. So, women can take the helms of their organizations and bring out powerful results. You have capacity for much more than you are probably doing right now.

Why do you need to get informed? Recall that Saul and his servant may not have expected much from the women they met on their way to finding the Seer. After all, what may you expect from a bunch of local women out to draw water? But the women knew more than pails and pots; it was just that no one ever bothered to ask them for directions. People may have written you off and said, "What does she know?" They fail to tap into the resources God has put in you. The first key to reversing that situation is by getting informed: educate yourself. Work on yourself because you will be a blessing to many. When the time is right, God will use all that He has put in you. The women Saul met talked about the city and showed Saul where the man of God was. "About this time," they said, 'this is where he goes; this and that are what he does." They knew all of those because they were well informed.

2. Watch and Pray
One way to stay spiritually alive is to constantly watch and pray. God has ordained us as women to be watchmen - or better put, watch-women - because we watch over our families. This is our peculiar role in the family, as can be seen even with female birds

and animals; they watch over their young ones protectively. Beyond our families and private lives, though, God expects the Christian woman to watch over all that He has committed to her. We are to watch over our cities; we are to change the spiritual state of our cities on our knees with fervent prayers. The prophet in Jeremiah 9:20-26 tells us, "Yet hear the word of the LORD, O women, and let your ear receive the word of His mouth; Teach your daughters wailing, and everyone her neighbor a lamentation. For death has come through our windows, has entered our palaces, to kill off the children-no longer to be outside! And the young men-no longer on the streets! Speak, "Thus says the LORD: 'Even the carcasses of men shall fall as refuse on the open field, like cuttings after the harvester, and no one shall gather them.' Thus says the LORD: "Let not the wise man glory in his wisdom, let not the mighty man glory in his might, Nor let the rich man glory in his riches; But let him who glories glory in this, That he understands and knows Me, That I am the LORD, exercising lovingkindness, judgment, and righteousness in the earth. For in these I delight," says the LORD. Behold, the days are coming," says the LORD, "that I will punish all who are circumcised with the uncircumcised- Egypt, Judah, Edom, the people of Ammon, Moab, and all who are in the farthest corners, who dwell in the wilderness. For all these nations are uncircumcised, and all the house of Israel are uncircumcised in the heart."

Jeremiah here calls for the wailing women. God was about to destroy the nation. The men having failed God, He called in the women for the rescue. They became the 'last card', the only hope for the nation. Jeremiah knew that if the women would wail before God, the land would be spared. And rising to the clarion call, the women came. This is one thing we know how to do very well, to wail and pray. It's just that many times we've been so hurt, and subsequently suppress this grace. We become unwilling to wail and pray, especially when we feel unrecognized and left behind.

God does not want us to come down with negative attitudes. We need to get back on our knees in prayer. You might not have attended a theological school, but go to 'Kneeology School'. It is the school of prayer. We know for sure that through prayers, God will do great things in our cities in Jesus' name. If we say no to prostitution in prayers, God will obliterate this evil from among our cities' womenfolk.

I found out that praying, even privately, to impact the streets where prostitutes are found does more than preaching on the pulpit. By preaching alone we don't get much done. It's slow. Of course, we have to evangelize; and there's time for that. But when we get on our knees and say, "Lord, no; let prostitution be wiped off our streets," then that's what we would see.

Similar laws could be passed against cults when we come together to pray. Prayer is one place we belong as women; and I believe that was the place of the women of Jeremiah's day. I believe they were praying women. Amos 6:1 says, "Woe to you who are at ease in Zion." It is by using the power of our tongue through prayers that we can change whatever is wrong in our cities.

3. Understand the Times and Seasons
You need to understand the times and seasons of your community and city because you have a portion in the land, and have a role to play in it. These are the days when organizations are looking for women to occupy positions but are not finding enough, because many women have relegated themselves to the backseat. The effect of this can be seen in Nigeria, in particular, where among the 36 states in the country, and of the 72 positions for governors and their deputies in the 1999 and 2003 general elections, only a sprinkling of women served as deputy governors. The only female governor in Anambra state came on stream temporarily in default of her boss who was impeached but later reinstated. At both the states houses of assembly and the National Assembly, the number of women was no better. Imagine what happens at their meetings, with so few women among a glut of men. They sure can do with some company!

I believe there are women reading this book who would occupy such positions. You can earn it and fill those positions. There are not enough women in the Senate yet. I read about one of them in the papers lamenting that politics costs money, and wondered where women can source the amount of money needed for campaigns and all that goes into politicking. But we can get around all that if the womenfolk got fully involved. The Bible says concerning the sons of Issachar that because they understood the times and seasons, their brethren were subject to their command. People flow towards those who have understanding and vision. Be a woman of vision, a woman going somewhere, and quite a number of people will follow you; then alone you can lead them into their destinies.

4. Choose the Right Company

How important is it to be in the right company? The women who Saul met were in company. Even in the case of Rebekah, she was not alone. It's just that she was the one that qualified. We need to move in company, team with women that are going somewhere, women of kindred spirit. Mix with one another, get to know each other's careers, flow together; do things together because there is power in synergy.

5. Go about Your Business Daily

Whatever your vocation or assignment is, do it conscientiously and consistently. Do it diligently and do it with humility. You see, those women must have been going to draw water every evening for God knows what number of years! But on this particular day, they met with opportunity. They gave Saul and his servant the direction to Prophet Samuel. I'm sure that by the time Saul met Samuel, he too must have said, "We understand you are such and such…" based on the information he received from those women. And Samuel may have retorted, "You are such an informed man…"

And when Saul finally became king, it is probable that he remembered those women. If he did not remember them, the opportunity was there for any of the women to walk into his palace and say, "Remember me? My friends and I were going to draw water the other day when we gave you directions to Samuel the prophet." She could land herself a lot of favor. That is how it works. So, keep doing whatever God has assigned you to do. Do it every day; do it diligently and consistently. Don't be tired of it, and do it with a humble spirit.

6. Don't Hold Back

As women, we should be ready to give at all times. I said at the beginning that women are givers. The word 'Eve' means life giver. Women are ordained to give. That is what God made us for. Don't hold back. Sometimes we are tempted to hold back, but don't hold back.

When Saul asked, "Is the seer here?" Those women could have decided not to answer him, and just go about their business. Or, they could have said, "He's here," and stopped there. But they took time to give him as much information as they knew. They did not hold anything back. They released everything that they knew. We must not hold back necessary information; we must not hold back our material goods and we must not hold back anything that God has blessed us with. We must not hold back in our career; we must teach others. The Bible says we must be apt to teach; teachers of good things. We must simply be a blessing by being on the giving end always.

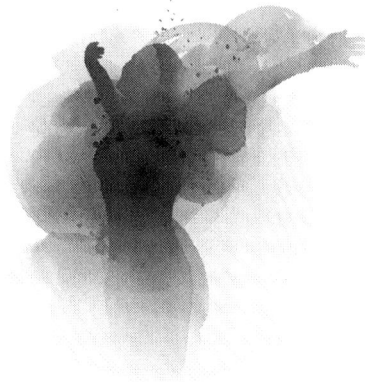

CHAPTER 2

BEAUTY FOR ASHES

Both Hebrews 6:9-10 and Esther 2:3-9 are two exciting texts on transmuting ashes to beauty.

"But, beloved, we are confident of better things concerning you, yes, things that accompany salvation, though we speak in this manner. For God is not unjust to forget your work and labor of love which you have shown toward His name, in that you have ministered to the saints, and do minister."[1]

"And let the king appoint officers in all the provinces of his kingdom, that they may gather all the beautiful young virgins to Shushan the

citadel, into the women's quarters, under the custody of Hegai the king's eunuch, custodian of the women. And let beauty preparations be given them. Then let the young woman who pleases the king be queen instead of Vashti." This thing pleased the king, and he did so. In Shushan the citadel there was a certain Jew whose name was Mordecai the son of Jair, the son of Shimei, the son of Kish, a Benjamite. Kish had been carried away from Jerusalem with the captives who had been captured with Jeconiah king of Judah, whom Nebuchadnezzar the king of Babylon had carried away. And Mordecai had brought up Hadassah, that is, Esther, his uncle's daughter, for she had neither father nor mother. The young woman was lovely and beautiful. When her father and mother died, Mordecai took her as his own daughter. So it was, when the king's command and decree were heard, and when many young women were gathered at Shushan the citadel, under the custody of Hegai, that Esther also was taken to the king's palace, into the care of Hegai the custodian of the women. Now the young woman pleased him, and she obtained his favor; so he readily gave beauty preparations to her, besides her allowance. Then seven choice maidservants were provided for her from the king's palace, and he moved her and her maidservants to the best place in the house of the women".[2]

Help from Above

There is something that I know is peculiar to women. We are known for looking for help in all kinds of places. So, let me start this exciting chapter by saying that every woman needs God's intervention in all of her peculiar circumstances. We expect and believe, as women, that God would do something new in our lives. In the presence of God you need no other.

Women typically get into situations where they need help. We are usually faced with challenges from our husbands and children among others. Life, it seems, has not been very fair to a lot of women. In both my church work and as a counselor, I meet a lot of women. And almost on a daily basis, I hear all kinds of things women go through. Some are traumatized by rape, and for some who end up becoming people's maids - with the frequent maltreatment that goes with that - life has not really been very fair. I know one thing, though, that God is interested in helping women. He made us. He said He would not leave us without help and comfort.

What breaks my heart, however, is that many women go to all manner of places except the right ones. Some erroneously seek spurious help from witchdoctors and cultists. Yet, it is only in God's presence that safety is guaranteed, because God will lovingly turn your adverse situations around. He wants to help you, and desires to bring beauty out of your life and move you to a higher level.

When I was writing this book, God spoke to my heart. He said, "I am a God of new levels. Remember not the former things, nor the old and unpleasant situations you have been through. See, I do a new thing. You can go to a new level altogether, a level that will have no correlation to your past; a level where you will not feel the pains of your past anymore. You must forget the past and forget the old. Embrace the new, for the new things I now declare. I bring you into joy and peace that passes understanding."

That to me, was like Joseph who said "God has made me to forget the toil of my father's house."[3] The message of this book is meant to make you forget every toil, every labor and hardship you may have been through, because God is bringing something new out of you; a beauty and blessing that will surpass whatever pain you have had before.

Step Out of the Past

We are never to get used to any abnormal situations despite the trepidation of stepping into something new. Of course, there will always be voices of discouragement. There will be oppositions too. But you must press on with God. When Peter stepped out of the boat to walk on the sea towards Jesus, of course, he must have heard negative voices calling from behind him to remind him of the potential parlous state of his wife and children should he drown. But he saw Jesus on a new level and was eager to meet Him there. I pray your own eyes will be opened to see the Master beckoning you to step into a new level too.

There is the old boat of complaining and complacency which we must step out of, and step forward into the dream God is impressing in your heart. This is where progress, peace and joy can be found; it is a new level of ideas that bring breakthroughs in life. May this be so in your finances, faith and family life. God is doing a new thing.

WOMAN

Paul says in 2 Corinthians 5:17, "Therefore, if anyone is in Christ, he is a new creation; old things have passed away; behold all things have become new." The Amplified translation says, "… the old has gone, see, I do a new and a fresh thing." You perhaps desire something fresh in your life. The Lord, I must assure you, is eager to bless you and get you into the place of blessing. And if you really understand His eagerness to bless you, then it is useless worrying about the challenges of life.

Get Set for God's Best

It's not that those challenges or adverse situations of life are not real to you. In fact, your peculiar case is probably very uncomfortable. However, if we knew the depth of God's love for which Paul prayed that we might comprehend the depth, the height, the breadth and the width, then we would be at rest because God gives us His best per time.

He gave us His best, His only begotten Son, Jesus Christ. Romans 8:32 actually says, "He who did not spare His own Son, but delivered Him up for us all, how shall He not with Him also freely give us all things [that pertain to life and godliness]?" From this scripture, we understand that God is not just interested in getting us saved from the powers of sin; thank God that is the starting point. Indeed, if you are not saved from the practice of sinning, you have no evidence that you have received Christ into your heart, nor the salvation of God. Right at this moment, God invites you to come straight to Him, ask His forgiveness and receive Jesus as your Savior. You would instantly be saved. But beyond receiving Christ and being saved, we must go further and press into the fullness of all that God has for us.

There are too many believers out there with heads hung low for various reasons. Christ is in their hearts, but their broken lives may have been due to wrong counsel from impostors. The pity is, even if God had put a beautiful gift in you, your actualization depends on the people you associate with. Some people are fire extinguishers while others ignite your fire when you come around them. I have a few of such people around me, who, when we share moments together, bring out the fire in me. Paul said to Timothy, "Don't forget the gift that you received by the laying on of hands."[4] He charged him to stir it up. When you are all alone, speak in tongues, read the Bible or come around people that can help ignite the fire in you.

Not Marked For Failure

The Living Bible has a very powerful translation of the text we read earlier in Hebrews 6:9-10. The background to the text is from verse 4.

"For it is impossible for those who were once enlightened, and have tasted the heavenly gift, and have become partakers of the Holy Spirit, and have tasted the good word of God and the powers of the age to come, if they fall away, to renew them again to repentance, since they crucify again for themselves the Son of God, and put Him to an open shame. For the earth which drinks in the rain that often comes upon it, and bears herbs useful for those by whom it is cultivated, receives blessing from God; but if it bears thorns and briars, it is rejected and near to being cursed, whose end is to be burned. But, beloved, we are confident of better things concerning you, yes, things that accompany salvation, though we speak in this manner."

Some believers do not see how this text applies to them personally. Backsliding is not God's intention for us. God has predestined nobody to be condemned. We are confident, Paul says, that you are meant for better things, things that come with salvation. I am confident that you are meant for better things. It does not even matter where you are right now. You might even feel that you are okay and comfortable, but that is still not the best. There's a better place for you because you are meant for better things.

Paul mentions the things that accompany salvation. After you are saved, you need the other things that come with salvation: health, divine healing, prosperity, fullness of joy and abundant life. "I am come," Jesus says in John 10:10, "that they may have life, and that they may have it more abundantly," not just life or average life, but abundant life - the best of life.

Great Joy Ahead!

We need to be expectant of good things always, because, really, the best is yet to come! See God doing something new in your life. See Him turning you on and taking you over. See Him releasing mighty favor upon your life. See Him bringing out beauty out of your life. The absolute truth is, there is beauty in your life that needs to be noticed.

Take the case of Esther, for instance. You may already know Esther. I particularly love this character in the Bible because she was favored by God. Favor, most times, is the difference between one person and that other person that seems so blessed. There is no better explanation of favor that is simple and strikes home as this. In her case, there was no rich father to start Esther on the path of greatness. This orphan girl had no great job with a fat paycheck, nor was her uncle a wealthy man. Considering her low beginning juxtaposed with God's favor on her life, none of us should have any excuses. We can seek and have God's favor to attain great things in life too. So, give no excuses.

The earlier you begin to tap into and walk in God's favor, the better, especially if you know you do not really have any natural help anywhere. Paul in our earlier text said, I am confident that you are made for better things. I believe this; and I'd like you to agree with me that you are meant for better things. You should desire better things that accompany salvation. Psalm 44:1-3 states, "We have heard with our ears, O God, Our fathers have told us, The deeds You did in their days, In days of old: You drove out the nations with Your hand, But them You planted; You afflicted the peoples, and cast them out. For they did not gain possession of the land by their own sword, Nor did their own arm save them; But it was Your right hand, Your arm, and the light of Your countenance, Because You favored them."

The last part of this text says, "Because You favored them." Because of favor, you will possess new territories and gain possession of lands, natural lands and lands from the realm of the spirit.

A land, you already know, typifies just an area or territory, but can represent your family too. It could represent your marriage, your career, and your peculiar field of endeavor. The Psalmist says you would gain possession of lands, areas in which the enemy seems to have occupied; things that rightfully belong to you but which the enemy seems to have sat on. This will not happen, as the Bible says, by sword, nor by power, nor by might; not by the flesh or physical fight or war would you take it back, but because of God's favor towards you. The question you should now ask should be: Lord, how do I get this favor? How do I tap into this favor? How do I walk in this favor?

Favor Tunes You Up

Favor makes you smell good, whether you use natural perfume or not. You just smell good. People are attracted to you and want to help you. People want to be associated with you. People are just kindly disposed to you. You are singled out of the multitude. This is favor. And that is your portion as a woman, especially when you recognize that favor comes from God. Acknowledge this and pray: "Lord, I know I can be favored by You. Bless me with Your favor."

When you are favored, you become the envy of people who wonder at what qualified you for where you are. You become a marvel, with no one able to analyze your life. You become a mystery. People wonder: "Is it her education or what?" They wonder, but you know in you that it's just the favor of God. That knowledge humbles you before God, and makes you appreciate and bow before Him in worship.

You see, the favor of God puts you beyond competition. Those who try to compete with you find, to their dismay, that their attempts are futile, because it's about favor. Life for you has become so beautiful; things are going well with you. You can't pretend about it. The sad thing, though, is many women do not bother to find out about the Source of divine favor. They choose rather to envy, backbite and pull down one another. "How does she deserve that?" Some women would complain out of defeat and low self-esteem. It takes greatness to appreciate greatness. You may not be up there yet, but if a fellow sister is in high position or on her way there, you need to give God praise for her life. The breakthrough of one woman should give hope that others will follow suit.

It is wrong assumption to think that some man out there is putting women down. I used to think so myself. I have since changed my mind, because God has changed me on the inside. It's true that women do suffer a lot. It's true that sometimes life doesn't seem to be fair; and most of the attacks on women seem to come from the opposite gender because everyone acts to the best of their knowledge per time. My counsel to every woman is, if anyone offends you or physically attacks or says all kinds of negative things to you, just tell yourself: That's how far he or she knows. Rather than be offended, pity will well up in your heart for the offender, because the way you act each time is a reflection of what you know. You act the level you know per time. The way you act today will not be the same when God brings you in contact with His word and changes you. You will not act next year like you did last year when something new has been deposited in you.

Bear No Grudges

Women need to forgive easily, because of our susceptibility to emotional trauma. In any case, the person you hold grudges against may have already repented in God's presence a long time ago about the offence he or she has done to you. And since God is near to them that are of a contrite heart and a broken spirit, He is very near to you when you demonstrate this humble attitude. He was near to David even though David committed adultery - a terrible sin. David even compounded his sin by killing Uriah, the husband of Bathsheba whom he had appropriated for himself. That was really terrible! Yet, God loved him because David understood favor. He knew where God picked him up - the backside of the desert. At another time, he said, "Lord, it's better for me to fall into Your hands than fall into the hands of man"[5]. We are told in Proverbs 30:21-23, "For three things the earth is perturbed, Yes, for four it cannot bear up: For a servant when he reigns, A fool when he is filled with food, A hateful woman when she is married, And a maidservant who succeeds her mistress."

Of the four things listed that the earth cannot bear in the scripture above, two or three point to the female gender, as the servant could be male or female. Verse 23 speaks of a hated, odious or hateful woman when she is married. When you have been hated or rejected, what happens is you have a tendency to pay back in the same coin. When you have been manipulated, rejected by someone you love or someone that is supposed to love you - this could be your father, mother, your husband or someone close to you - you have a tendency to be manipulative, to do the very same thing to others. Verse 21 says that the earth cannot contain such a person or people. The earth is disturbed or disquieted, the earth is not healed; it is troubled when a hateful woman is married.

This scary implication should serve as warning to you if you are single and presently live in rejection, hate and all that. You need to open yourself up and let God heal you before you get married, because if you get married in that state, then an explosion is bound to occur. When you are still single, you bottle up a lot of things, but the moment the opposite gender comes in, something devastating happens; and because of this the earth is disturbed.

I believe sincerely that we need healing for both genders. This is something we need to pray about regularly, especially in our nation, that the Lord would bring healing between men and women so we would complement each other. Let there be healing; let there be understanding; let there be love, and let there be appreciation.

Gender Struggles

The Women Lib thing, as I understand it, is scripturally unnecessary. The Bible gives no support for women to struggle for some unfounded liberation. We are already liberated in Christ. We don't have to try to prove any point. Jesus has already proved the only point there is that He loves us more than we can ever imagine.

The woman caught in adultery in John 8, was at the verge of being brutally stoned to death by religious bigots. But she was taken to Jesus. Thank God she was taken to the right Person. Those religious men thought Jesus, being a man, would join their band to condemn the woman. But they saw the God-side of Jesus. They told Him what the law says, that anyone who committed adultery should be stoned to death. Rather than answer them, the Master kept quiet. Did you ever wonder where the man was, with whom the woman was caught in the very act of adultery? After all, if truly she was caught in the very act, as her accusers said, was she doing it alone? Their accusation in John 8:1-3 did not say she was a suspect. So, if she was caught in the very act and she wasn't doing it alone, where was the man involved? Apparently, he had gathered his clothes and bolted away, and they let him go because he was one of them.

Gender war, I've come to understand, is an ancient battle. Beginning with the very first couple, Eve and Adam, this battle has raged on. After they sinned and the woman in an attempt to wriggle free from the steady punitive gaze of God, pointed to the Devil as initiator of their sin. She said it was the Devil that made her do it. It's an old excuse, you see. Apparently hurt by her accusation, the Devil, I believe, targeted the woman from then on to harass and afflict her. The coming of Jesus has changed all that, though. I believe we are liberated. Jesus is our strong bulwark and impenetrable defense. He is the Defender of the weak. So, if ever you feel harassed or threatened by the enemy, go to the right Person: Jesus the Lord.

The Psalmist also speaks of a maidservant who succeeds her mistress. When you talk about a hated married woman, I remember Leah in the Bible. I don't want to go into her story here. But Leah, the first wife of the Patriarch Jacob, was cheated. She didn't beg to be married, but she was caught between a deceptive father called Laban and an equally sly husband before God changed Jacob. She was hated because Jacob didn't plan to marry her. He loved Rachel. The Bible says, "when God saw that Leah was hated, He opened her womb."[6]

Look, you may have been hated or rejected, but that is the very qualification for you to enjoy the favor of God. You, however, need to have a positive self-esteem. It's not right for you to say, *Let people go on hating me*. Understand that you need to embrace God because you are hated. If no one loves you, run to God. Don't be neutral. Don't be complacent, doing nothing, nor hate those who hate you. Don't just say, 'This is not fair; the God that I serve will fight for me,' when as yet, you have not even come close to this God.

We also have a maidservant who succeeds her mistress. Does that remind you of Hagar, who was maidservant to Sarah? Sarah had given Hagar a little room. She had felt, 'Since I'm unable to have a child, let Hagar step in.' Sarah loved Abraham so much she wanted to help God bring His prophecy to pass concerning her husband. But that was wrong. If God has spoken something, just stay still and act on what He has said He would do. All you need do is watch out for opportunities and stand still, and before your very eyes you would see God's promises come to pass. It may seem to delay and look like God is late in coming, but God will never be late.

Sarah said to her husband, 'You are still fertile. You can have my maid.' She trusted and loved this maid as a daughter. But when Hagar conceived she changed and became arrogant against her mistress. Sarah must have realized, though too late, that she had been hasty in allowing Hagar onto her matrimonial bed. The lesson for us is not to run ahead of God. Let's have love and compassion for one another. I just don't know how that compassion flows, but I know it flows from God.

Hard Tackles as Challenges

I was with a very powerful Nigerian woman of God sometime ago at a meeting. We were preparing for a prayer program when she said, "Look, Nigerian women have not been fair to me." I knew what she was talking about because I knew where she was coming from. She added though, "but I love Nigerian women." She recounted an incident once at the airport on her way out on a foreign trip. At the Customs she was passed by a male officer, but a female officer there would not let her go despite recognizing her as a reverend woman of God. The woman officer so frustrated her that day, she was befuddled.

That women experience hard tackles from fellow women is common. But rather than begrudge one another, let our compassion be released towards one another. This compassion is not a gender thing. It is not a women society of sort, nor a women liberation thing. It is about the love that Christ has for us. We must understand that He loves us. He doesn't love us less than the He loves men. I believe that the minds of many people reading this book are being changed to appreciate womanhood.

One woman was telling another woman about a friend of theirs who had just given birth to a child, and she asked, "What did she have this time around?" Apparently, another friend of theirs had just given birth to a child. Her friend answered, "She had a boy." On hearing that, her partner gave a boisterous shout in jubilation. Their joy for a boy child was quite revealing. It demonstrated that there would be less excitement were the child a girl. And that speaks volumes about the low esteem many women have of themselves. It stems from a wrong mindset. But understand, it's about us as women. Those ladies were jubilant because their friend gave birth to a boy, not a girl. They communicated what was in their heart that a male child was better than a female child, yet they were both females. Can you see what I'm getting at? It's about us and the change that should take place in us.

Woman, this is about you going before God and saying, "Lord, I may not be strong on the outside, but I know You help the helpless. You use the weak things of this world to confound the wise. Use me, Lord, to make an impact." The process here is not about contending with your husband to be recognized. He may be doing things that are really unfair to you, that if were to bring your case before someone, they would probably blame him and agree with you that he is at fault. But you sure do not intend that others should verbally assault your husband in public. That will not change the situation. When you, however, go to God and say, "I have no power of my own, Lord. You alone can change the heart of any being: the hearts of kings are in Your hands. You favored Abigail. You are the God of Hannah. You brought Esther, a disadvantaged orphan girl into a palatial life. You are the God of Ruth who in the midnight of her life met a Boaz, a favored husband."

When we prayerfully read the word of God, we are encouraged. God urged Israel to look at their father Abraham and at their mother Sarah. Look at the people God has blessed in the Bible. Move near contemporary women who are close to God. Move with people who Paul, in the Bible, described as written epistles, seen and read by all men. Let them know your peculiar area of challenge. For all you know, they may have handled similar situations in their own lives, and could offer godly counsel that will set you on your way up again.

Lessons from Shushan

I'll like to deal specifically now with God's favor on Esther. The background to her story is in Esther Chapter One. The king had dethroned Queen Vashti because she had poor character and was out of favor with the king. She had publicly spurned her husband. Her place as queen was subsequently declared vacant. The courtiers began to look for who would be the next queen. It was like a beauty pageant. Esther 2:4 says, "Then let the young woman who pleases the king be queen instead of Vashti. This thing pleased the king, and he did so."

You may look at the king in terms of a natural man or as God. Jesus is our King, the King of kings and Lord of lords. You can look at the king as your husband. The king's men said, "Let the woman who pleases the king be queen."[7] Yes, beautiful ladies from around the domain of the king, including Esther, were brought in and were given necessary cosmetics and attires they needed to enhance their attraction to the king. They were there for months to prepare for the day they would be paraded before the king. Yet, only one of them would have to please the king. The vital lesson here is in verse 7.

"And Mordecai had brought up Hadassah, that is, Esther, his uncle's daughter, for she had neither father nor mother. The young woman was lovely and beautiful. When her father and mother died, Mordecai took her as his own daughter."

Mordecai became Esther's mentor. What Naomi was to Ruth, Mordecai was to Esther, and even much more. He spoke into her life and saw potentials in her. He saw things she did not see in herself. He did not suppress her gifting. He did not see her merely as an orphan or as a good-for-nothing-girl, whose worth was only to serve as a maid.

When Mordecai heard about the 'opportunity' at the king's court, he grabbed it and recommended Esther, filled the necessary forms, and put her in for the beauty competition. He brought her up and must have seen that her beauty was deep within, beyond her skin. She was beautiful outwardly, and also possessed the inner beauty of righteousness which God imparts on us when we come into Christ. Mordecai knew what God had invested in Esther. He knew what he had nurtured.

By helping Esther overcome her low self-esteem, Mordecai gave her the needed confidence to go into the competition gracefully. She might have thought that no one would desire her, especially being a Jewess. The Jews were not even supposed to be part of that competition. "Just go ahead," Mordecai must have urged her on. And she did. Verse 9 says, "Now the young woman pleased him, and she obtained his favor; so he readily gave beauty preparations to her, besides her allowance. Then seven choice maidservants were provided for her from the king's palace, and he moved her and her maidservants to the best place in the house of the women."

While Esther was yet to get before the king, she found favor with Hegai, the king's servant. His role was crucial because he was to determine who got to go into the presence of the king. If Hegai said, 'You there, I don't like your face. You're out of this competition," that contender's fate was doomed. It was Hegai's role to do the screening and to give the ladies the things to enhance their preparations.

Humility as Password

The preamble to Esther's meeting with the king is similar to common experiences in modern job markets. Sometimes, on your way to favor, you are required to pass through certain persons whose approval is important. This could be the concierge, or the personal assistant or secretary to the person you want to meet. You may have the required appointment letter to see their boss, but as 'gate-keepers' to their boss, they reserve the right to let you in or frustrate your move. You may have the interview notice, for which you have been short-listed and billed for 9a.m., yet you need humility to get past the gate. If the guard at the entrance feels blighted and chooses to delay you until 11 o'clock, your protest would not help matters.

The interview would have been done with by the time you get in. All you would hear from the interviewer would be "Sorry, you came late." It is so important that you humble yourself before everyone you meet along the way, because you do not know who will be the helper of your destiny. It does not matter how that person looks. He may be a guard, that's true, but the entrance is his territory; and you must conquer that territory before you move to the next. God is near those who are humble and favors them expressly.

Esther found favor with the chief servant, who gave her things speedily. This is interesting. There are things that are meant for you; things that accompany salvation. There are things that should accompany your salvation; things you are entitled to as at today. Look, it's not a thing of pride to say you want your things. It's not a thing of pride to go before God and say, "Lord, my things; give me the things that are due to me, things You promised in Your word. I want my things." This is not pride. In fact, it is humility when you agree with the things God has said about you. And when you use your gift in life, you are rewarded.

When you have what people are looking for, they will not care whether you're a man or woman. That is the realization I came to have. I did not think that way before. I knew I had some gifts in me. I knew what God was telling me too, but it was like the thing in me was not finding expression. I was busy blaming my frustrations on others other than myself, when all I needed was to wait for the timing of God.

The Footprints of the Messiah

Jesus, for instance, for the first thirty years, merely went to the synagogue where they gave Him the Bible as a lay reader. Yet He was the Messiah! He would sit through all their boring services. He would be given the book, which He would read. And as His manner was, He would go and humbly sit down after reading. At no time did He say, "Pity, you don't know who I Am?'" Jesus was a standard example on humility!

See your time of tutelage as a trial and a test. See God watching to see how you would respond. I have come to discover that when you have the answer to what people are looking for, they will come for you. It does not matter whether you have everything as yet. You might be selling fries and hotdogs on a street corner. Those who are hungry won't say, "It's a woman, therefore her fries are no good." No. So long as you have what the people need per time, they don't care whether it's a man or woman in possession of it. They will come to you. And this is a very needy world. We need all kind of things, from food and clothes down to encouragement. It's therefore not *about 'I'm too short, tall, fat* or *slim.'* First, locate your pearl or treasure in your field of endeavor. Go for it, and people will come after you. Then life will pay you in return for what you offer. God would ultimately pay you because He is the one who put the gift in you to both use and live by it.

When to Pray

One day I went before God to ask for my own things. Going before God need not be going down on your knees in prayers. Prayer is not a one-time affair. Rather, it should be a lifestyle. You can talk to God as you walk down the street or while driving or in the public bus. Just tell Him, "Lord, I'm here about this thing." That is prayer.

In fact, that was what I did. I told Him I wanted my own things. I had not even seen the text in Esther in this new light as at then. I suddenly realized that I was also entitled to some things. You know, aside your husband blessing you with things, you should have your own things too, your own things no matter how little they may be; your own little shop, your own little business which should grow. Thank God we do not despise days of little beginnings.

I prayed that when parcels of gifts come to us, some envelopes should come in my name aside those addressed to my husband. Well, it is peculiar with us women, I suppose, that when it's your own money it's really your money; but when it's his money it's our money. We're all culprits in this matter! This is one reason I enjoy being a woman. Indeed, if there were reincarnation, I would still like to come as a woman despite all the rejections and the constraints attached to womanhood. The blessings, the dividends still pay much more than what we seem to lack.

The envelopes started to come when I also discovered my area of gift and started to give of myself. It's not a matter of competition that I can preach as much as my husband preaches. If I weren't called to preach I wouldn't preach. I encourage you to discover your own area of gifting, whether as a banker, or as an entrepreneur or whatever else you are called to do. God would make yours unique because of His gift in you. People would come to your shop and bless you. You would recognize the favor of God. That's why I said life pays you for what you have to offer.

For now, God may not allow you to do some form of secular work. He may, for the time being, consign you to being a nursing mother, to stay with your kids because some children need their mothers longer than others. God, who knows the destiny of each child, knows whether this child needs a working mother or one at home for a certain time in its life. As with grown-ups, children could be extroverts or introverts. One child may need its mother to be home till he or she is five years old while another might need the mother till they are twelve. We just need to flow with God.

Blessings for Mothers

One of our sisters in church wore a beautiful hat one Sunday that I greatly admired. "That's a beautiful hat," I said to her. She then said her husband went to minister somewhere and the people there sent that hat to her with a bottle of perfume. She wasn't there. They didn't even know what she looked like; they had just prepared a gift for her. For the fact that her husband came and he had a wife somewhere, that was her own honorarium, not for preaching, but for being at home with the kids.

God knows how best to favor you. So it's okay to say, "Lord, give me my things." And I see God delivering our different things to us, things that make for beauty because, as the text says, Hegai gave Esther her things for beautification or beauty preparations. Not only did he give her all the things that she needed, he did so speedily. He readily gave her, not grudgingly.

You see, when you are favored, your blessings will not be delayed. Hegai eagerly gave Esther her things and moved her and her maidservants into the best place in the house, away from all the other ladies who came for the competition. God has kept the best place for you too. He readily gave her beauty preparations besides her allocated allowance. Count whatever you have today as an allowance. That was part of the things I had in mind when I told God to give me my things. Aside the allowances, I also wanted the real things that are meant for me; the things that accompany salvation - not just allowances or a salary, not things that are here today but are not tomorrow. I wanted tangible spiritual things. These are the things that make for inner beauty. My prayer was, *'Bring them out of me, O Lord; impart them to me and let them come to the limelight.'* Inner beauty is what makes one to find favor. Esther 2:15 says, "Now when the turn came for Esther the daughter of Abihail the uncle of Mordecai, who had taken her as his daughter, to go in to the king, she requested nothing but what Hegai the king's eunuch, the custodian of the women, advised. And Esther obtained favor in the sight of all who saw her."

Some may say, "Well, Esther didn't go that far on her own." Yes, her uncle connected her. But God's connection is the most powerful influence for getting things done in our favor. Heaven is God's throne and the earth His footstool. What other influence can be any more stupendous than that? He sits in the heavens, but the earth is His footstool where He exerts His influence among men. You may not have connections anywhere among men, but your heavenly Father has the longest reach, and you can be rightly connected.

Win Over Your Enemy

In the same verse 15 quoted above, Esther requested for nothing but what Hegai advised and gave her. Yet she obtained favor in the sight of all who saw her. God wants you to smell good and obtain favor with those who meet you; they will just have to love you. It's either they like you or they don't. But you see, people who do not like you make you quickly define your scope. You do not need to make everyone like you anyway. Seek to please God, then He will make men to seek you. The Bible says, when your ways please God He makes your enemies to be at peace with you.[8] Therefore, if you please God but some people are not pleased or happy with you, then they are not meant for you, because you are not sent to everyone, and everyone is not sent to you.

Don't waste your time trying to court the favor of everyone; it's no use. That you can please only a few people at a time makes your assignment very easy. For instance, I know I'm sent to those who hear me or read my books, and I speak like one sent to them. Esther was favored by all who saw her. Verse 17 says, "The king loved Esther more than all the other women, and she obtained grace and favor in his sight more than all the virgins; so he set the royal crown upon her head and made her queen instead of Vashti." If God would do this for an orphan girl, moving her to a palatial life and transforming her rags to riches, I see God doing much more for you.

But see her secret in verse 9. "Now the young woman pleased him…" Esther pleased Hegai. It is probable the other maidens came with a proud look knowing that Hegai was not the one who would make the selection after all. He wasn't the king before whom they were to parade. In other words, he wasn't the main man.

Beyond Physical Beauty

Agreed, Hegai must have perceived that Esther had inner beauty. But Esther's beauty was not everything. Peter admonishes us in I Peter 3, that our beauty should not only be outward adornments. How we appear outwardly is important; it is good to look real good because, as women, we are creatures of beauty. Looking good makes us feel good. But this should not be an outward affair only; we should have inner beauty too. We are to beautify ourselves with the Word of God, with meekness and humility. That is what Peter says is inner beauty. These holy qualities will reflect on the outside. You may not have many clothes today, but if you have inner beauty whatever you wear will fit you just well.

Please God Always

Beyond pleasing the servant, Esther pleased the king ultimately and got his favor. Beyond any of His servants, we should seek to please God our King and Maker. It is in pleasing Him that we get His favor. Our main assignment as Christians in this life, is to please God ultimately. This provokes God to bless us with things we have not even asked for at that particular moment.

We attract God's favor when we please Him in worship, when we are humble and depend on Him. Do not lean or trust your own understanding. Acknowledge the fact that, but for God, you are nothing. You may have a first class brain or degree and have become very successful where others have failed. It is God that keeps you alive and allows you to have breakthroughs in life. There are people with equal brainpower, and who attended the same schools and institutions as you, but who trudge the streets abysmally. So whichever way you want to look at it, your present success is still traceable to God. Hebrews 11:6 says, "Without faith it is impossible to please God." Please God with childlike faith. And you know, God knows and perceives faith. It is as we please Him that it becomes well with us.

The Pauline Strategy

If you are married, please your husband. In 2 Corinthians 11, Paul speaks of how good it is to be single, because he was single and really enjoyed remaining so. It gave him time to serve the Lord. As he said, "Woe is me if I preach not the gospel."[9]

He deliberately chose to stay single because of his own peculiar destiny. At one point he said, "I also have the power to lead about a sister."[10] That is, he could also have proposed marriage to a sister and got married just like the other apostles. *But because of my destiny and the burden that is laid upon me concerning the gospel,* Paul thought, *Why marry.*

In any case, if he had married, the wife would probably have left him; and that would have been a 'but' in his life. Today we can't find a 'but' in the life of Paul. He wrote two-thirds of the New Testament with no account of blemish in him. But if he had been married, the wife most probably would have thought he was dead already on hearing he was stoned, bitten by a snake, ship wrecked, put in prison and ready to be executed. Not knowing that God raised him up from under the pebbles and that an angel came and delivered him from prison, Paul's wife would probably have gone on to marry someone else after some time because when someone's husband dies, the Bible says you are free to re-marry.

Can you imagine Paul resurfacing after two years not knowing his wife had remarried! She'd say, "But we thought you were dead." His children would have taken the brunt of their absentee father and perhaps become wayward, because he would not have been there for them. It was this peculiar calling of Paul that made him advise that let the married man please his wife and let the married woman please her husband, for those who are married are saddled with that burden, or so it seemed to him anyway; that you have to manage between pleasing God and pleasing your spouse.

Dividends of Godly Marriage

Those who please God should not find it difficult to please their spouses. The starting point, as 2 Corinthians 6:14-17 warns the Christian, is marrying right: Christians are not to marry unbelievers. No unequal yoke can work together until they are agreed or made the same by the new birth experience. So, if you are going into marriage, think deeply about the choice you are making. I tell you, when you please your spouse there are dividends. When I please my husband, I know how he blesses me. The man's care for his wife is not supposed to be a conditional love, but we are human, and respond to pleasing overtures.

Let's please God and He will speedily deliver into our lives things that make for beauty. I see you move to a new level even as God has declared. I see your eyes open to see opportunities around you. I see you smelling good. In places you have been rejected before, I see you being accepted because there's a new you coming out of the old self. You have a new understanding of who you are. Something new has begun to happen in your life.

CHAPTER 3

OIL
OF
JOY

We have reached a point in this book where I plead with you to please indulge my passion, because I want to focus mainly on Ruth, one of my favorite characters in the Bible. I suggest that you read Ruth 3:1-18 to have an appropriate understanding of this extraordinary woman. The text reads: *"Then Naomi her mother-in-law said to her, "My daughter, shall I not seek security for you, that it may be well with you? Now Boaz, whose young women you were with, is he not our relative? In fact, he is winnowing barley tonight at the threshing floor. Therefore wash yourself and anoint yourself, put on your best garment and go down to the threshing floor; but do not make yourself known to the man until he has finished eating and drinking. Then it shall be, when he lies down, that you shall notice the place where he lies; and you shall go in, uncover his feet, and lie down; and he will tell you what you should do.*

So she went down to the threshing floor and did what her mother-in-law instructed her. And after Boaz had eaten and drunk, and his heart was cheerful, he went to lie down at the end of the heap of grain; and she came softly, uncovered his feet, and lay down. Now it happened at midnight that the man was startled, and turned himself; and there, a woman was lying at his feet. And he said, "Who are you?" So she answered, "I am Ruth, your maidservant. Take your maidservant under your wing, for you are a close relative."

Then he said, "Blessed are you of the LORD, my daughter! For you have shown more kindness at the end than at the beginning, in that you did not go after young men, whether poor or rich. And now, my daughter, do not fear. I will do for you all that you request, for all the people of my town know that you are a virtuous woman.

Now it is true that I am a close relative; however, there is a relative closer than I. "Stay this night, and in the morning it shall be that if he will perform the duty of a close relative for you-good; let him do it. But if he does not want to perform the duty for you, then I will perform the duty for you, as the LORD lives! Lie down until morning.

So she lay at his feet until morning, and she arose before one could recognize another. Then he said, "Do not let it be known that the woman came to the threshing floor." Also he said, "Bring the shawl that is on you and hold it." And when she held it, he measured six ephahs of barley, and laid it on her.

Then she went into the city. So when she came to her mother-in-law, she said, "Is that you, my daughter?" Then she told her all that the man had done for her. And she said, "These six ephahs of barley he gave me; for he said to me, 'Do not go empty-handed to your mother-in-law.'" Then she said, "Sit still, my daughter, until you know how the matter will turn out; for the man will not rest until he has concluded the matter this day."

Time to Recover Lost Grounds

The Bible puts it simply: "Weeping may endure for a night, but joy cometh in the morning"[1]. The Living Bible translates the verse this way: Weeping may go on all night, but with the morning comes joy. Women, I must demonstrate to you, are creatures of joy. You were created joyfully by a joyful God, and you were received in joy. It doesn't matter what you are going through right now or whatever the devil has made of your situation, God ordained joy for the woman from the beginning. Not only is joy your portion, you are also made to be a carrier of joy.

In Genesis, it was God that decided to make the woman, not as an after-thought, but as part of God's original plan. He brought the woman on the scene because He knew this world could be a better place, because man would not be complete without her. Adam did not have to lobby God to give him a woman. God had it in mind that the woman should be on the scene. She was made joyfully, not grudgingly.

And when God brought the woman to the man, Adam said, "This is bone of my bone."[2] He seemed to say, 'Where on earth have you been? You don't look like any of the animals and things I have seen.' Eve was received joyfully. Her husband was happy at her coming. The world is happy that you are around, woman. Don't look at your situations and circumstances and feel that because you are experiencing rejection here and there, therefore you are not needed or that you don't have a purpose around here.

Let's go back to the beginning and see the mind of God about the creation of the woman, how He intended the woman to be a creature of joy, a distributor and giver of joy. The joy in a woman's life is contagious as the rays of the morning sun. The sun signals a new day, a new beginning with fresh hope. Like the sun, the woman holds special promises for the man and for the world.

A New Level

God is the God of new levels. He does not want you to remember the former things, the things of old and situations that you have been through. He charges us not to "remember the former things, Nor consider the things of old. Behold," God promises, "I will do a new thing…"[3]

God promises us joy and peace that is beyond human understanding. Joseph testified that God made him forget the toil of his father's house. This new level does not come without oppositions. Whenever one attempts to step into new things in life, there are usually voices of discouragement. When Peter was about to step out of the boat of 'confinement and containment' with the other apostles, some may have attempted to discourage or keep him in rather than see him walk on water as Jesus called him to do.

You may have been surrounded by people like that who cannot imagine you moving forward or making progress. You do not have to stay in the boat of complacency with them; step out into a new level as Peter did. Be bold to step into a new level of peace, of joy, of ideas that would bring breakthroughs in your finances, marriage and life generally.

Forget the past. Forget everything that had happened to you up till last night. The morning has come. As the Lord says, "New things I declare."[4] That is the word of God; believe it and embrace it. Let me humbly say that God has sent me like a Mordecai to an Esther, and like a Naomi to a Ruth. He has sent me to speak into your life, to bring instruction, to help to birth or sow the seed of what He wants to do, so that the questions of your heart would be answered. Like the Virgin Mary, you may ask, "Lord, how shall these things be?" I tell you, only believe, and it shall come to pass.

God at Work

Let me give you a background to Ruth 3:1-18, which we read at the beginning of this chapter. The first two chapters reveal Ruth as a woman who, after the midnight of her life, received eternal joy. Ruth was from Moab. She was not from Israel, the lineage of Abraham, Isaac and Jacob; the nation God had blessed. She happened to be married to one of the sons of Elimelech who was in covenant with God, a seed of Abraham, but left his country because there was a terrible famine in the land. He went into this strange land with his wife, Naomi and their two sons, Mahlon and Chilion. Both sons got married in Moab, one to Orpah, the other to Ruth, both Moabites. It so happened that Elimelech and his two sons died in Moab, leaving Naomi and her two daughters-in-law as widows.

Having lost her family, Naomi decided she had had enough. Life, it seemed, had been unfair to her. She lost her husband and two sons in a strange land. She resolved to return to her own country, Israel.

She suspected she would be mocked because when she returned to her country, the people would most likely say, "Well, you went in search of greener pastures and returned worse than you left here." But she chose to brace up and return to her country all the same. She kissed her daughters-in-law good-bye. The first one, Orpah, kissed her and stayed back in Moab, but "Ruth said: "Entreat me not to leave you, Or to turn back from following after you; For wherever you go, I will go; And wherever you lodge, I will lodge; Your people shall be my people, And your God, my God. Where you die, I will die, And there will I be buried. The LORD do so to me, and more also, If anything but death parts you and me." When she saw that she was determined to go with her, she stopped speaking to her."⁵

Ruth was a woman of insight and faith. She was an "unbeliever" but had come to believe in the God of Elimelech and Naomi. She believed that though Naomi appeared destitute, there was hope with her if she joined her destiny with Naomi's. In the natural, it would have benefited her more to stay in her country, re-marry there and move on with her life but she was ready to follow Naomi. She resolved to take the God of Naomi to be hers too, and Naomi's people her people. God honored the faith of Ruth and adopted her. The God of Israel became the God of Ruth.

In Ruth 3:3, Naomi became her instructor. Whatever Naomi told Ruth to do she did. She said to Ruth, "Wash yourself and anoint yourself, put on your best garment and go down to the threshing floor; but do not make yourself known to the man until he has finished eating and drinking." When God is set to move you to a new level you'd have to put on your best. From this chapter alone, we can see some keys about putting on your best. Naomi asked her to put on her best and not appear shabby. The same applies to you. Don't go in your rags. Don't go like one begging for something. Put on your best because you don't know when your opportunity will meet you.

Best is relative, though. Your best may be different from mine. Most women have what we call "bottom of the box" clothes. Those are special wears we put on once in a year, at Christmas perhaps, or those special outings. They are in the class of our best, and those are the sort of things which heighten our profile with those we meet.

Don't ever belittle any situation. Here are the keys:

1. Put on Your Best All the Time

Make it a habit to look good always. Don't belittle the mid-week services in your church and appear casually, leaving your best dresses for Sunday services alone. Don't presume your office is of any less importance than attending a party where fabulous clothing tends to make a greater impression. Put on your best per time, and God will keep changing your best. Naomi said, put on your best and Ruth did.

In verse four of the scripture above, Naomi says, "Then it shall be, when he lies down, that you shall notice the place where he lies; and you shall go in, uncover his feet, and lie down; and he will tell you what you should do." When God is about to move you to a new level, you will begin to notice things that you did not notice before. When you begin to notice something new, this could be from the word of God. Get ready! God wants to do something, and has put you on notice.

Naomi told Ruth, "You shall notice the place where he lies." That means, as you go, open your eyes and expect your opportunity to meet you. "You shall uncover his feet and lie down and he will tell you what to do." Psalm 23:2 says, "He makes me to lie down in green pastures; He leads me beside the still waters." We have to know how to lie down, to lie down in God's presence.

2. Wait for God's Still Voice

Of course, we are in the age where everybody is always up and about. We are either going somewhere or coming from somewhere. But we all need to lie down to hear something from God. When young Samuel, in the night, heard his name and ran to his mentor, Eli, he asked: "Did you call me?" Eli said, "No I didn't call you, go and lie down." He went back, but heard his name again and ran to Eli, because there was no one else in the house of God at Shiloh. And again Eli told young Samuel, "Go and lie down again." When you lie down, you could hear something from God; you could hear what He wants to do in your life and in the lives of those He would send you to.

Finally, Eli said, "Lie down again, and if you hear the voice again, it must be the Lord, because it's not me; then say, Lord, speak..." Then God began to speak to Samuel about his life's mission. I see God instructing you about any adverse situation you may be in right now. And beyond that, I see God revealing your purpose in life to you. When your purpose is in place, your joy will be in place. The reason many of us are having bouts of depression, and are happy one day but down the next, could be because we've not really discovered our purpose, and have not begun to walk in the fullness of it. But I believe that even now, God will move you to a new level and open your eyes of understanding. You will discover your purpose and embrace it. After that, God would begin to deal with you differently. And you will begin to see things differently.

3. Beyond Listening

In Ruth 3:5, Ruth assured Naomi saying, "All that you say I should do, I will obey." And in verse 6, she went down to the threshing floor. You see, it's not enough to hear instructions from God; you must be ready to take action and do what God says. Ruth went down to the threshing floor. The Bible doesn't say she stayed, argued, rationalized or tried to reason it out. She went down to the threshing floor and did according to all her mother-in-law instructed her. In any case, if she was not ready to obey her mother-in-law, why did she follow her to Israel in the first place? I believe you are ready to obey God and go all the way with Him.

In verses 7 and 8, Boaz, the subject of the plan of Naomi, having eaten and drunk, laid down to sleep. But at midnight, he was startled when he found a woman lying at his feet. For the men reading this, you can imagine how you would feel if you woke up in the middle of the night to find a woman lying beside you? Boaz was a type of Jesus in the sense that Jesus is our Kinsman and Redeemer. Jesus is happy when He finds us at His feet, whether at midnight or any other time of the day. We come to His feet to learn of Him and to receive from Him.

Boaz turned at midnight and there lay a woman at his feet. There are some good things about the midnight, you know. Though usually dark and symbolizes the twilight of our lives and is full of challenges, yet it is in the night that you grow the most. Plants also grow in the night. During the day, they receive sunlight just like we receive the Word of God when we are conscious or at personal Bible study or church meetings. But it is when we lie down at night to sleep that we stretch the body inadvertently and grow in the process.

James 1:2 says, "My brethren, count it all joy when you fall into various trials." This is saying that we should count it all joy when we are in the midnight of our lives. Reckon it all joy, James says, because it will become joy when the morning comes.

God gives us a song in the night and turns our mourning into dancing. It is always good to be alone with God. We lose nothing but gain all important things when we are alone with God.

4. Know Who You Are

When Boaz was startled from sleep on seeing the woman, he asked her: "Who are you?" The woman answered, "I am Ruth." You must be able to know who you are, not who they say you are; and not what people have called you. I see this over and over in the Bible.

To Jacob, the angel said, "Who are you and what is your name? Yet the angel knew he was Jacob. When God asks you a question, it's because He wants to know if you know who you are. He wants you to know the level you are at, because you must first admit where you are before He can tell you where He is taking you.

Jesus said to His disciples, "Who do men say that I am?" They gave Him all kinds of answers. "Who are you?" Boaz asked the woman, and the woman said "I'm Ruth your maidservant; take your maidservant under your wings because you are a close relative."

Don't let your life be controlled or dominated by other people. God didn't create us to be controlled by other people. He made us to be controlled and led by His Spirit. He put His Word in us and gave us His Spirit. Even God does not control us against our will. He put His Word in us and expects us to respond to His leading. Don't let your life and values be defined by what other people have said about you. Know who you are in Christ. Have an understanding of who you are and move on in life.

5. Be Empowered to Fear No More

In Ruth 3:11, Boaz said, "And now, my daughter, do not fear. I will do for you all that you request, for all the people of my town know that you are a virtuous woman." He said do not fear, nor can you afford to entertain fear like before. It's a new thing that God is doing altogether. He does not want us to "remember the former things of old"⁶. "Behold I do a new thing," He says. In about 365 places in the Bible, we are told do not fear. "Be not afraid," He says, "I am with you, I am your God; I will strengthen and uphold you."⁷

Boaz said, "I will do for you all that you request, for all the people of my land know that you are a virtuous woman." Have a good reputation and be known for something good. Show kindness to people. Speak good words into people's lives. Do good things and embrace a worthy cause. Ruth's reputation went ahead of her as "a virtuous woman". Of course, the fact that she came from her own country with Naomi who was already looking like a failure, was something to her credit. It was a good deed that her daughter-in-law came to live with her for the rest of her life.

Verse 14 says that Ruth "lay at [Boaz's] feet until morning, and she arose before one could recognize another. Then he said, "Do not let it be known that the woman came to the threshing floor." She held on until morning. Don't give up at midnight. Hold on till daybreak. Hold on till your morning comes. Ruth waited and held on till the morning; she arose before anyone could recognize her. If you wait till the morning, surely God will cover all your shame and reward you openly. God will connect you with the helpers of your destiny. I believe so much in that.

He connected Ruth with Naomi, even when Naomi didn't look promising. He also connected Naomi with Ruth, in a way, because at the end of the day, Ruth turned out to be a big blessing to Naomi. He connected her with Boaz. God is in the business of connecting people. He will connect you with people for your own destiny as well as theirs. So it's not just about you. Of course, you'd be blessed in the process, but it's about God blessing you and making you a blessing to others. It's about you tasting and seeing that the Lord is good as well as saying, "Such as I have, I give unto you."

"Bring your shawl," Boaz said to Ruth, and he gave her some barley and sent her away blessed. God is a God of comfort. He's a beautiful God. Jesus says, "I won't leave you comfortless."[8] He will never leave us comfortless. Even in times of trials and temptations, there is always an area of life where we see God's blessing. Rather than complain about delayed expectations, we are to look at those other areas of blessings and say, "Lord, thank You. If You could do this, You'll do the rest." God expects us to look at our shortfalls and yet retain inner joy. He expects us to look at Him and have joy. For the fact that you are in Christ, you have hope. Only those without Christ lack hope altogether.

6. Watch God Work for You

When Ruth got back to her mother-in-law in the morning, Naomi asked, "Is that you, my daughter?" Ruth told her all the man had done for her and handed over the things Boaz had given her. Then Naomi said, "Sit still my daughter, until you know how the matter will turn out." There is a time to lie down, a time to act and move; there's also a time to be still and know that God is God. There is a time not to help Him bring about what He wants to do. There's a time to stay and just watch. "Sit still, my daughter until you know how the matter will turn out," Naomi said, "for the man will not rest until he has concluded the matter this day." God will not rest until He has concluded what concerns you also.

What need do you have today? God will not rest until He has concluded and gotten to the end of it. Naomi said that to Ruth because she knew Boaz, who was a kinsman. She understood Boaz, which was why she asked Ruth to go to him at midnight and lay at his feet. That was like saying, "Go to the feet of the Master; I know him." "They that know their God," Daniel 11:32 says, "shall be strong and do exploits." You've got to know God. I know Him and that is why I'm recommending Him to you. Go to God; go to His word. Stay at His feet and hear what He will tell you to do; and whatever He says to you, just do it.

The mother of Jesus, in John 2, knew her Son. She knew the power He carried by revelation, not because she had seen Him do any miracles as yet, because as at that time, Jesus had done no miracles yet. Like everyone else, Jesus, with His disciples, was invited to this wedding. Though He was God, in His humanity, Jesus attended the wedding, perhaps like everyone else, to have a nice time. But the celebrant soon ran out of wine. His mother, knowing that Jesus was both man and God, knew He would make a difference. She therefore said to Him, "Look, they don't have wine anymore, please do something about it." But He said, "Hey mom! It is not yet my time. It's good you know Who I am, but don't expose Me yet."

It's not yet time, or so He thought. I see Mary as a kind of instructor here in the natural; a kind of mentor because she knew all about the Son even before Jesus was born. She was a helper of His destiny. But He seemed to say to her, "I know you know Me, but don't expose Me here." However, she was working according to the time of God. So she kind of said: "Okay, You know You can do it; so do it."

Through with the Son, Mary went to the attendants at the ceremony and said, "Whatever He says to you, just obey." Those are the same words that you need to move to a new level: Whatever Jesus says to you, just obey. Whatever instruction comes your way from the Lord, just obey. We see that Mary would not even take a no for an answer. Even if God was not ready to perform the needed miracle, her faith and persistence compelled the Son to take action. She insisted it was time.

In Revelations 12:6, we see the dragon running after the woman. Pursuing the woman is an old practice. At the beginning, when Adam and Eve sinned and God came into the Garden of Eden to inquire what man had done, Adam pointed at Eve and said, "It is the woman You gave me." He readily blamed God for giving him the woman. He readily blamed the woman for eating the fruit first, and then giving him to eat. God turned to the woman, "Why did you eat of the fruit?" And the woman sheepishly pointed at the Devil and said, "It was the devil." God now turned to the devil, who rather than answer God directly, seemed to face the woman instead, and with a vengeful gaze said, "Woman, why blame me for this?"

That seems to me the signal of a special antagonism against the woman. Not that the devil is not after men too, but he is especially after the woman because his own punishment was given to him with respect to the woman's seed. "And I will put enmity Between you and the woman, And between your seed and her Seed; He shall bruise your head, And you shall bruise His heel."[9] And from that time onwards, the devil began to look around for the woman's seed that would bruise his head. He knew the child would come from the descendants of Abraham through Sarah. He first thought it was Moses. And in an attempt to kill baby Moses, before he could grow to bruise his head, the devil instigated Pharaoh to order the killing of a countless number of Jewish children. He did the same thing through King Herod when Jesus was eventually born.

You see, the devil understands prophecy, and knows the word of God as well. But he is not omniscient; and as such, does not, many a time, know the timing of God's good purposes and plans. His strategies to thwart God's plans often do not tally with God's all-knowing thoughts and timing. That's one reason you would constantly escape every plot of the devil. I tell you, the devil won't understand how God would hide you; and like a mystery, you would be hidden from all his evil schemes in Jesus' name.

"Now when the dragon saw that he had been cast to the earth, he persecuted the woman who gave birth to the male Child. But the woman was given two wings of a great eagle, that she might fly into the wilderness to her place, where she is nourished for a time and times and half a time, from the presence of the serpent. So the serpent spewed water out of his mouth like a flood after the woman, that he might cause her to be carried away by the flood. But the earth helped the woman, and the earth opened its mouth and swallowed up the flood which the dragon had spewed out of his mouth. And the dragon was enraged with the woman, and he went to make war with the rest of her offspring, who keep the commandments of God and have the testimony of Jesus Christ."[10]

Satan disgorged something from his mouth like a flood to sweep off the woman. But the earth opened up and swallowed up the flood that the dragon spewed out to cause the woman to slide so he could lay his hands on her and destroy her. As the earth helped the woman, so God will cause you to be helped marvelously. Woman, know that you are favored. Have the mentality of a favored person as you walk about. Do not be worried about the machinations of evil people. God will cause the earth to help you.

It's a reality that evil people abound everywhere, but you need not bother yourself about them. It's true that evil schemes originate from the devil and that he finds expression through evil people to attempt to harm us, but do not be so conscious of evil to the point that you are disturbed. Yes, I know there is evil in the world. I'm not one of those who see life as a bed of roses. But the Bible says, in Psalm 74:20, "Have respect to the covenant; For the dark places of the earth are full of the haunts of cruelty." There is cruelty in the world, and we have to admit that. But be conscious of the fact that you would be helped by God.

The earth opened up. It was necessary for God to open up the earth to swallow up the flood of the dragon so the woman would be helped. Understand that everything on this earth, whether they grow out of the earth as food, or meat from animals, God intended them all to be a blessing for you. Be conscious of the fact that God has put people on this earth to help you. Be conscious that you are favored of God and that His blessing is stronger than any curse that may have been placed on your life or over your lineage.

7. Discover Your Pearl and Stop Worrying

Let us go back to the story of Naomi. She told Ruth that Boaz would not rest until he had concluded the matter the same day. The Bible says, "The end of a thing is better than its beginning..."[11] I see God concluding the affairs of your life beautifully. Your worrying will not change a thing. God has set the time, and I believe that the time is now. As Matthew13:44-46 states, you need to discover your pearl.

For you to have joy, you have to discover your pearl and treasure. I mentioned earlier that knowing your purpose in life is the greatest prayer you can pray for yourself after you've come to know the Lord. "Lord, let the eyes of my understanding be opened."[12] That's how Paul prayed for the Ephesian Christians in Ephesians 1:17-19, which says, "That the God of our Lord Jesus Christ, the Father of glory, may give to you the spirit of wisdom and revelation in the knowledge of Him, the eyes of your understanding being enlightened; that you may know what is the hope of His calling, what are the riches of the glory of His inheritance in the saints, and what is the exceeding greatness of His power toward us who believe, according to the working of His mighty power." Our eyes of understanding need to be opened so that we would know what God has in stock for us; what He wants us to do, that we may walk and live our lives according to His will.

It's a terrible thing to think you are doing the right thing when you are doing the wrong thing. But when you discover your purpose, as Jesus says, it is like a hidden treasure in a field which when you find, joy comes into your heart. And this is joy that causes you to rearrange and reorganize your life. The one who found such treasure, Jesus was saying, sold all he had. This means that he put aside every other thing he was doing.

My Own Testimony

When my husband came to know the Lord while in college, he asked the Lord, "Where is my treasure, so that I may put my heart there?" Because the Scripture says where your treasure is that is where your heart would be also.[13] Indeed, if you have put your money in a bank, your heart naturally will be inclined to the bank always. If your money is under your bed, that is where your heart will be. Then of course you won't be able to sleep, as you would constantly fear that robbers would come. But if your money is lodged in a bank, the fear of robbers becomes the bank's problem, not yours.

My daughter, at one time, had a slight fever and was feeling quite ill. She could not go to school. What I did, then, was pray for her, administer some medication and off I went to the office. I could stay there and worry over her condition, and feel so bad. But I was there in the office feeling happy and having a nice time. All I did after that was call home to find out how she was doing. I just said to the devil, "You aren't tired of this trick?" You see, I've come to discover that every time I was to go and preach somewhere, something would always pop up, especially with my daughter. The devil was fond of making her feel ill. But not anymore! Today she's alive and bubbling, bouncing around the whole place. The devil intended to disturb me and make me fret about her health. It was supposed to be a sign of discouragement. But no way!

When you have discovered your pearl, the Scripture says, you would buy the field and leave every other thing aside. I discovered my pearl in the preaching of the Word of God and I put aside architecture, which was my training. I put aside every other thing because I've found where my pearl is. And that reminds me of Proverbs 31:16. It talks about the virtuous woman that considers a field and buys it.

Divorce? Perish the Thought!

Buying landed property? That brings a new dimension to the on-going discourse. I said so because as a woman I can buy land. And that was a discovery for me. You too can buy land. But if you are married, it's not for you to hide your possessions from your husband. You do not buy a piece of land and keep it from your husband. Some women do that in the event of a divorce or separation from their husbands. But that is unchristian. The future is nothing to fear about.

As Christians, we do not live in fear; we live in faith. God would send you ahead at times to preserve your family. The land he provides for you to buy might just become handy to bail your family out of trouble in the future. You however should not go about bragging: "I bought the land, not my husband." You have to be humble because God resists the proud and is very far from pompous people.

Profit from Virtue

About the virtuous woman, Proverb 31:16 says, "She considers a field and buys it; From her profits she plants a vineyard." Now, what has buying a field got to do with making profits? Simply buying something does not in itself turn it into a profit? For instance, if you buy a piece of land, it does not become a profit immediately. Of course, you have spent some money, you have made an investment, but that does not look like profit on its own. But if you leave that plot of land for some years, you could resell it or build a house on it, which you can put out for rent from which you can earn profits. You can then plough back your profit into further investments.

What the Scripture is simply saying is that one door leads to another. When you have discovered where your treasure is, you leave every other thing. That is what I believe the English mean when they ask, what is your field of endeavor? What is your field? What is your chosen field? We could say the same for careers too.

If you find something that is your territory, stay there. Don't look about for things you do not have a calling for. Look at your field; only through that field will you make a profit. Your life will be profitable. As the text says, you will have joy.

CHAPTER 4

HEALED AND SENT TO THE NATIONS

For a long time, I cried to God, "Lord, heal me." I ached in an area of my life and for this reason, I needed the touch of God. I have found that women, in many cases, need healing. This may not be physical healing. Many a time, when we need physical healing for an injury, we go to a doctor, and it's treated and dressed up. But there are inner wounds that no one can see. What ointment, bandage or plaster can be applied to your emotions? Even beyond that, we have a spot called the heart. There's the physical heart that pumps blood and people have had surgery on that part, which can be opened up with the knife of a surgeon. When the healing is done, it leaves a scar. Only the balm of Gilead gets down to the heart of hearts and heals without physical surgery or a scar.

It is Jesus Christ who performs such a healing, and that is the kind of healing we need for a broken heart.

The Joyful Song of the Barren

Patiently go with me now through Isaiah 54:1-17, and see the interesting exultation of the barren who breaks into singing.

"Sing, O barren, You who have not borne! Break forth into singing, and cry aloud, You who have not labored with child! For more are the children of the desolate Than the children of the married woman," says the LORD. Enlarge the place of your tent, And let them stretch out the curtains of your dwellings; Do not spare; Lengthen your cords, And strengthen your stakes. For you shall expand to the right and to the left, And your descendants will inherit the nations, And make the desolate cities inhabited. Do not fear, for you will not be ashamed; Neither be disgraced, for you will not be put to shame; For you will forget the shame of your youth, And will not remember the reproach of your widowhood anymore. For your Maker is your husband, The LORD of hosts is His name; And your Redeemer is the Holy One of Israel; He is called the God of the whole earth.

For the LORD has called you Like a woman forsaken and grieved in spirit, Like a youthful wife when you were refused," Says your God. For a mere moment I have forsaken you, But with great mercies I will gather you. With a little wrath I hid My face from you for a moment; But with everlasting kindness I will have mercy on you," Says the LORD, your Redeemer. For this is like the waters of Noah to Me; For as I have sworn That the waters of Noah would no longer cover the earth, So have I sworn That I would not be angry with you, nor rebuke you. For the mountains shall depart And the hills be removed, But My kindness shall not depart from you, Nor shall My covenant of peace be removed," Says the LORD, who has mercy on you.

O you afflicted one, Tossed with tempest, and not comforted, Behold, I will lay your stones with colorful gems, And lay your foundations with sapphires. I will make your pinnacles of rubies, Your gates of crystal, And all your walls of precious stones. All your children shall be taught by the LORD, And great shall be the peace of your children. In righteousness you shall be established; You shall be far from oppression, for you shall not fear; And from terror, for it shall not come near you.

Indeed they shall surely assemble, but not because of Me. Whoever assembles against you shall fall for your sake. Behold, I have created the blacksmith Who blows the coals in the fire, Who brings forth an instrument for his work; And I have created the spoiler to destroy. No weapon formed against you shall prosper, And every tongue which rises against you in judgment You shall condemn. This is the heritage of the servants of the LORD, And their righteousness is from Me," Says the LORD."

The World at Your Feet

To the woman reading this, let me tell you that nations are in you. Those were the words of God to Rebekah, the wife of Isaac. Rebekah was troubled and uncomfortable with the state of her pregnancy, and sought to know why her situation was so. God told her, "Two nations are in you. You are about to birth greatness."

When, as women, we go through seasons of discomfort, pains and rejection, it brings us to the place of prayer where we can cry to the Lord for help. "For a small moment have I forsaken thee," God says in verse seven of the text above. This is only a manner of speaking. God spoke that way because that is the usual terminology we often use as humans. We sometimes feel as though God were far away from us, and has left us without help. But the truth is that God is ever present with His children. Even Jesus, when He was on the cross said, "My God, My God, why have You forsaken Me?"

Even if it were true that God sometimes appears to 'abandon' us in hard times, it is usually for a short moment of time to enable us learn by experience how to be a comfort to others in the future. That's what Apostle Paul tells us in 2 Corinthians 1:3-4, "Blessed be the God and Father of our Lord Jesus Christ, the Father of mercies and God of all comfort, who comforts us in all our tribulation, that we may be able to comfort those who are in any trouble, with the comfort with which we ourselves are comforted by God." It is therefore not what we are going through now, but Who is in it with us. God shares in the tribulation of His children.

There are things you go through now, which, if you would be patient with God, will turn out for your good in the future. But some become impatient and bolt away into making some decisions that they later regret. If only I knew what God was doing in making me have those painful experiences, they later would say. But they have hastily taken certain actions in fear, when like Jesus, they could have endured the present inconveniences and not have spurned God. That's why in James 1:2, it says we are to count it all joy when we fall into all kinds of trials, knowing it would work patience in us and bring about a great and solid woman in you.

Sorrow Will Not Last

There's a scripture I would like you to read with me. God gave me a powerful revelation from it some time ago. See it in Psalm 30:1-7.

"I will extol You, O LORD, for You have lifted me up, And have not let my foes rejoice over me. O LORD my God, I cried out to You, And You healed me. O LORD, You brought my soul up from the grave; You have kept me alive, that I should not go down to the pit. Sing praise to the LORD, You saints of His, And give thanks at the remembrance of His holy name. For His anger is but for a moment, His favor is for life; Weeping may endure for a night, But joy comes in the morning. Now in my prosperity I said, "I shall never be moved." LORD, by Your favor You have made my mountain stand strong; You hid Your face, and I was troubled."

The immediate thing that struck me here is that after the long hours of sorrows and prayers, there must follow the long life of joy and singing. That's the first of three instructions God laid in my heart from this scripture. Sing, and there is no two ways about it. In the first verse of Isaiah 54, where we read earlier, the sorrow of the barren woman turned into joy and singing. This may or may not be physical barrenness. Whichever the case, it says sing if you are going through some form of dryness in your life or business right now. The Psalm says, "I cried out to You, And You healed me. O LORD, You brought my soul up from the grave."

Well, it does seem the case that if one's soul is in the grave, one would be hard pressed to sing. But we sure can sing when we make our story His story. The word 'history' should be translated 'His story.' That was the way this Psalm came to me. God wrote the scripture before you were born. He wrote the story and when it was time, He allowed us to be planted in our mothers' womb.

That's why He told Jeremiah, "Before I formed you in the womb I knew you; Before you were born I sanctified you; I ordained you a prophet to the nations."[1] This was God's response because Jeremiah perhaps was thinking, *'How could He just spring me up like that'* as he continued to give God excuses. "I did not just call you on the spur of the moment," God said, 'I have planned this very thing before you were born; it's in the script. So now, step out."

If we are sensitive to God and walk with Him, there are things He would tell us that would sound far-fetched and way beyond us. That is often the case with many Christians who, though convinced that God wants them in the ministry, hold back in fear of the unknown, and bring up a lot of excuses. But no, we are to go forth and obey the calling of God in our lives.

You Won't Die

One thing about an action story is that, whether you watch or read it, the star actor never dies. Every other person may die, but it gets to a point you begin to reason that the star actor can't. And you know, we are stars. You can't die before your time. And guess what, we are all acting our different parts in the full package. We all have different stories, but ultimately, it is His story. We may live our different lives, but all our stories are going to become history. And you know what, history is - the past in concise record. By tomorrow, today would become yesterday and tomorrow would be today. How we live today is all part of it. You, perhaps, sometimes feel, *'O Lord, are You angry with me? I don't even feel Your presence. Are You there? It seems You have left me alone.'* His response will always be that His favor is for life. Remember, "Weeping may endure for a night, But joy comes in the morning."[2]

Has He Forsaken Me?

You know, when you look back and can see how you've been tossed to and fro, and how God has helped you over time, you come to that point where you can really say, "I won't be moved by anything anymore; it's not worth it." It does not mean trials will not come again, but you now can see that there is no point in fretting about anything. You now know, that at the end of the day, God would show Himself strong on your behalf. The Psalmist says, "I shall never be moved. LORD, by Your favor You have made my mountain stand strong."³ The Amplified version says, "Lord, by Your favor You established me like a strong mountain."

In Isaiah 61:3, God promises those that mourn in Zion, "beauty for ashes, The oil of joy for mourning, The garment of praise for the spirit of heaviness." The purpose is so "they may be called trees of righteousness, the planting of the LORD, that He may be glorified."

That's why we share testimonies, you know. Over time, we come to know how to stand on our own with God on our side. We become strong and no more the weak and feeble babies we used to be, when we would weep and cry over little things. We have become strong on the inside, as solid women; women that can absorb things, making others to marvel at the grace of God in our lives.

Who is a Widow?

Back to the opening verse of Isaiah 54, which says: "Sing, O barren, you who have not borne! Break forth into singing, and cry aloud, you who have not labored with child! For more are the children of the desolate Than the children of the married woman," says the LORD." My understanding of this scripture, is that more than children for the desolate, the rejected or the lonely, something greater is in the offering for the barren than being - so to speak - "happily married." Of course, there's nothing wrong with us being happily married. If anything, that's what we all should be. Verse 6 further states, "For the LORD has called you like a woman forsaken and grieved in spirit, like a youthful wife when you were refused, says your God." Join that to verse 4 which says, "Do not fear, for you will not be ashamed; neither be disgraced, for you will not be put to shame; for you will forget the shame of your youth, and will not remember the reproach of your widowhood anymore."

God dropped this in my spirit some time ago when I was meditating on this scripture and it made me ask: Who is a widow? As I began to meditate, I saw that there are different kinds of widows. A woman whose husband is dead and has not remarried is a widow. But the Lord added a new dimension to that. He said, "Do you know that there are many women that their husbands are alive but appear dead?" These are husbands who are physically in the house but are of little use, or so it seems. He is there in the flesh, but does not take any form of responsibility in the family, whether financial or sexual. He might have even broken all the marriage vows, yet he's still there 'on paper' or in the house in a separate room. He might even be there on the same bed, yet it's like he's not there. That woman can be identified as a widow. She's an emotional widow. Some women are in that state right now or have been through it. But you know, God, as the Scripture says, is a faithful Husband and always expects us to recognize that He is our first Husband. Therefore, whether your human husband is performing well or not, we are married to God.

Many others have what used to be a beautiful and happy marriage, but they have come to a point where the oil of gladness is finished, and the man seems aloof in the area of intimacy and care. While in courtship, he used to send you cards, but he does not seem to care anymore, making you feel a sense of loss. Remember, the only One who is faithful and never disappoints is God. He is your real Husband.

A Jealous God

There is this thing about us women, when our husbands are doing well, and walking with the Lord; we feel cool about him being what we really expect. Sometimes, we experience the opposite once our intimacy with the Lord diminishes. Perhaps not everyone feels this way, but it is true that many women tend to forget God in times of extreme comfort.

It is not that you have backslid from the Lord, only that you just can now afford to spend all the time with your husband and things are just blissful. But when there's a problem, not even necessarily with his business but on his person, when his attitude and behavior changes. He suddenly has changed from what he used to be; only then do such women begin to sing emotional songs unto God. But the thing is, God is a jealous God.

Sometimes, God allows little afflictions so that you can run to Him. He desires to have that intimate relationship with you always, as do partners in love. God is looking for true worshipers. He does not want us to get to the point where we do not need Him.

He sometimes allows certain levels of affliction even in times of extraordinary wealth, so we can remain close to Him. For those who suffer afflictions of poverty and need, when eventually God has turned things around and you become very comfortable, God desires that you frequently look back to all you've been through and constantly fall on your knees to praise Him.

It's not only when things are not fine with us that we should run to God; in good times as in bad times, we should humble ourselves before God. He is sovereign, and cannot be judged.

You Will Expand

Leah, the first wife of Jacob is like the desolate woman, while Rachael, her sister and Jacob's second wife, was the loved one. But when God saw that Leah was hated, He opened her womb and blessed her with children. However, she could not see that as God's love and be content; she struggled and clamored for the love of her husband whom she and her father had previously connived and hijacked from Rachael.

I remember also the story of Jabez in 1 Chronicles 4:9,10. He prayed that God would enlarge his coast. "Help me so I would not grieve anymore," he said. "Bless me also," he fervently prayed. You too, perhaps may have wondered, *'Why is it that every step I take is wrong?'* God says in Isaiah 54:2, that you go ahead and enlarge the place of your tent. You have prayed, you have toiled, and all night you have cried. Now you go forth and enlarge the place of your tent.

Many times when we think we don't have anyone to help us, we tend to reduce our vision. It may have been a 'six-by-six' vision, but we reduce it to 'two-by-two' because we say, "I don't have a wealthy uncle or a ready husband to help." God is saying, enlarge the place of your tent for you shall expand to the right and to the left, and your descendants will inherit the nations. It's more than just about you; it's about what God wants to do in the future through your children.

Promise for Our Children

I think a healed woman would better train a child and lead that child in the way the child should grow than a woman who is not yet healed. So the earlier we get our acts together, the better for us, so that our children would be like arrows in the hands of a mighty man[4]. So get it; if you are not going to the nations yourself, your seeds should. They should inherit and possess the nations. And, talking about nations, it might be a geographical location or ethnos as the Greeks call ethnic or people of common values. It is therefore about professions, about gender. God might be sending you into the nation of the medical profession. You might be in the ministry for women or children. God is sending you to an ethnos, a particular ethnos.

You know, when you are from a particular ethnic group, you understand them. That is why you have to come from them to minister to them. It's like doctors or lawyers. They speak a particular language and understand one another. If for example, God is going to use you to minister to broken women, do not think that you will not go through anything yourself. If God is going to use you to comfort the barren or those who have delays in child-bearing, do not think that you will not go through a period of barrenness yourself. One thing that I know is, whatever you may suffer in preparation for your ministry is only temporal.

Stop These Excuses

There is a way we could force God to hasten His Word to perform it.[5] Some of us are earning salaries, but God is saying no; you are to be an entrepreneur. Meanwhile, we give excuses about where to raise the capital. Do you want to wait till you are fired from that job before you move?

Sometimes the devil does just that, and God allows him, if only to force you to hear and obey Him. Being fired from your job does not mean you are out of God's will; only that your fear tends to delay the manifestation of your destiny. What could have taken the children of Israel just forty days took them forty years. Where were they coming from? Between Egypt and Tel Aviv now by air is about three hours. So going by foot would be about forty days. Yet, they were going round in circles. If you look at the map you will see that the distance is not as far as it seems; but they spent forty years reaching the place. Whatever situations you are in right now, ask God what you stand to gain from it. *'What is it You're trying to show me, Lord?'*

Damning the Spirit of Fear

"Sing!" God says in Isaiah 54; that's the first instruction I got from the text. The second is in verse 4, "Do not fear, for you will not be ashamed; Neither be disgraced, for you will not be put to shame; For you will forget the shame of your youth. And will not remember the reproach of your widowhood anymore." We should be able to confidently issue fear the divorced bill for life.

There is this joke about the spirit of fear and the spirit of death. The spirit of death was crying to the devil, their master, that there were so many accusations against him killing people. He protested he wasn't the one that killed all of those that died, but the spirit of fear did. He explained that when fear enters, death is the result.

And that's very instructive to the intent we should not be afraid. Don't be afraid to take the step you are sure God wants you to take. Did God say to enlarge? Take the step of faith and enlarge, because there are no two ways about it.

Don't be swayed by the fall in the exchange rate or bad trading at the stock exchange. Don't reduce your investment, because doing so would mean cutting down on your vision. I advise you emphatically, do not cut down on any vision; except God did not say a thing in the first place. If He did, then do not try to help Him fulfill His word. God's word to you per time is an opportunity for you to shine. Even when things appear to get rough, it is still an opportunity to shine.

God is good and He is bringing increase to us because He has brought healing to our lives. But whether you feel healed or not, just move. By the time you get there, you will be healed.

Reward for Perseverance

Three women got up very early one morning to go to the tomb of Jesus, some three days after He had been crucified. As they went, they remembered that a very heavy stone had been rolled over the tomb. They had their spices to embalm or do some service on the body of Jesus but were faced with the challenge of the heavy rock, which they felt sure on their own they couldn't roll back. Yet they went on. They had a purpose.

The surprising thing in the story is that they did not turn back though confronted by a seemingly daunting problem. These are the kind of women God wants us to be. They did not turn back but kept going though aware of the problem. But alas! When they got there, the stone had been rolled away miraculously by an angel.

After they had entered the tomb, though, they were bemused, as they did not see the Master's body. The other women chose to return to the city but Mary Magdalene, one of the three, was very curious about the whereabouts of her Lord's body. While she mourned, the Master appeared. It is to her credit that she was the first to see Jesus after His resurrection. He revealed Himself to her. This could be your season of revelation, but you must be ready to take steps, to go ahead and enlarge your coasts. Put away excuses. Just move ahead. If the word of God is in you, then tap into God's resources and move ahead. Don't let anyone put you down. Make sure though that you are really in partnership with God and that you let nothing unholy come between you and Him, because that will remove the seal of His covenant with you. Give God what He deserves as your first Husband. Serve Him more than you serve your human husband.

Identifying Your Ministry

You know, in the beginning, God put man in the earth for a purpose. He said, have dominion and take over the earth. Yours may not be core pulpit ministry *per se*. But we are all in some kind of ministry, because we are all sent to minister to one another in the earth. Yours may not be about any of the five-fold ministries as in Ephesians 4:11.

There are other gifts. God may have called you to be an entrepreneur in some business, or a teacher, and has asked you to start a Day Care center right from your home because He wants to do something amazing and raise a peculiar kind of children through you. They need not be children from your own womb. Go ahead with the plan. Serving in some good purpose in the earth is one way of taking dominion in the earth.

Remember that God did not make any airplanes or jets and did not even build any houses. He just put Adam there and gave him the minimal worries and said, have dominion. But see what man has made of the earth since then.

From the rivers we have built dams, tapped electricity, and so much more.

So find your own place. God has called us to make life more comfortable for everyone on the earth. So whether you are a carpenter, a fashion designer or whatever else you are doing, make life more comfortable for humanity. If you make chairs for people to sit on, do it so well to glorify God because that is what will give God pleasure when you are doing what He expects with excellence. This is a form of worship. If you have been called to comfort people, like I'm doing through this book, then, that is your own place. Yours might be to put comfortable clothes on the back of men and women. These are all ministries in some way.

Not Just the Kitchen

Some women erroneously see the kitchen as their ultimate. Thank God for the 'kitchen ministry'. I am a very family-oriented person, but I am still on the go for the Lord. Being a stay-at-home mum to raise children is an important ministry too. It is work because no time spent to prepare your seeds to inherit the nations is a waste. The earlier you begin to tailor and train them for how they will take over and inherit the nations, the better. Knowing that your children will rule and lead the nations helps you to train and prepare them now. That will determine how well they will do later when they begin to make huge decisions and many other important issues later in life.

We should not be frustrated by present situations in government, but should believe God to see our children take over as presidents and CEOs. We must however train them well, else they would end up being just as obnoxious as some rulers as we loathe today. God forbid that our children should sponsor legislations disempowering senior citizens, all because they don't know any better or had parents who were wicked to them. God has given each parent an assignment to bring up and train their children in the Lord. This is important also, for ourselves, because they are our future.

CHAPTER 5

THE FRUITFUL BRANCH

In Gen. 41:51-52, Joseph called the name of his firstborn Manasseh, saying, "For God has made me forget all my toil and all my father's house." Then, he named his second son, Ephraim, saying, "For God has caused me to be fruitful in the land of my affliction. God has caused me to be fruitful in the land of my affliction." Likewise, I want you to know that you are divinely fruitful when you remain faithful even after going through the valley, through afflictions, through contrary, and through adverse situations.

What made Joseph so fruitful? The answer is simple. You are a rod and branch of fruitfulness. How do I know? I know because God has destined everyone to be fruitful. You may not know it but I pray the eyes of your understanding are opened to know this truth. God has destined you and I to be fruitful.

God Ordained Our Dominion

You are not barren, even if you are married without children at the moment. You are a "waiting-mother" or "waiting-father". Everyone has to wait for something at some point in this life. I don't know about you, but I know that there are things that I'm still waiting on God for. Regardless, I'm fruitful because God said so in Genesis 1:28. I believe God wants you to know that you are already fruitful, but He wants you to move into the realm of multiplication. Never forget that God ordained our dominion. That's what He told me - to move into the realm of multiplication, the realm where I multiply myself. That's exactly what you do in business, you multiply yourself. The process doesn't end with fruitfulness. The multiplication cycle has to go on. Understand, though, that there is a power of fruitfulness and there is also wisdom for fruitfulness.

Painful Pills

For many, it is difficult to reconcile going through hardships with walking in dominion. When God's word came to Moses, it brought him and Aaron criticism and affliction even though they were called by God. I love the prophetic word in Numbers 17:8, which says that, "Now it came to pass on the next day that Moses went into the tabernacle of witness, and behold, the rod of Aaron, of the house of Levi, had sprouted and put forth buds, had produced blossoms and yielded ripe almonds." This is the power and wisdom of God on display.

The wisdom of God is the Word of God. He has called and chosen you too. Jesus tells us, "You did not choose Me, but I chose you and appointed you that you should go and bear fruit."[1] Earlier in verse one, Jesus had said, "I am the true vine, and My Father is the vinedresser."[2] If you are connected to the Vine, you'll know that it is the Father pruning you through adverse situations. The Father is testing and trying you so you can produce more fruit. If you understand Him, you would be joyful in affliction. I have come to accept faith as my lifestyle. If you live a lifestyle of faith, you will go through affliction with joy knowing fully well that it will end in your victory. When you are in the valley, you will have that assurance that you will eventually get to the mountain top. And I can tell you from experience, victory is sweet.

So do not let anyone tell you that you won't go through any hardships. You surely will. But when you come out, you will be as gold. Paul said, "I'd rather grow in my afflictions so that the power of God would rest upon me."[3] When I sense the power of God radiating around me, it's because I've gone through some things, but stayed connected to the Vine. If you stay connected to Jesus as a branch, you will bear fruit. But if you are not bearing fruit, go into God's presence and He'll tell you what to do.

When God Gives His Word

God called Moses and He called Aaron as well but the children of Israel persistently complained and murmured against them. When they were happy, Moses was their beloved 'pastor', but when faced with challenges, they would complain about everything, literally accusing him for his effrontery in bringing them out of Egypt. "You should have left us in Egypt to continue our servitude,"[4] they would bicker against Moses and Aaron. They did not understand God. They knew His acts but they did not know His ways.

You see, the word of God has creative power. That is why I do not need to see fruitfulness in my life before knowing that I am a fruitful woman. Some years ago, just before I got married, God spoke into my heart. He said, "You are blessed among women and highly favored." And like Mary, I knelt and said, "Lord, how could these things be?" Because it did not look like it at the time. About two years later, the Lord said to me, "You are a mother of mothers. Women, who are even older than you, will come to you for counsel." I did not look like it then, but that was the word of fruitfulness and I received it. The important thing is for you to know that you are a fruitful person, whether you look like it or not, because there is fruitfulness as an occurrence as well as fruitfulness as a state of being.

I am fruitful as a person. You are fruitful when you have the Word of God in you. At another time, God said to me, "Wherever you find yourself, you will flourish. You will be fruitful." When you operate on certain principles, for example, having the word of God in your heart, you see yourself through the lens of the word and you stop operating at your level of understanding. You believe what God says you are. Jesus, in John 15:16 says, "You did not choose Me, but I chose you and appointed you that you should go and bear fruit." Jesus said every branch in Him that does not bear fruit, the Father cuts down. God hates barrenness with a passion because He said in the beginning, "Be fruitful." Identify with that.

Aaron's Miracle

In the Bible, God used the rod of Aaron as a sign. It literally put an end to the complaints of the Israelites. Numbers17:8 says, "Now it came to pass on the next day that Moses went into the tabernacle of witness, and behold, the rod of Aaron, of the house of Levi, had sprouted and put forth buds, had produced blossoms and yielded ripe almonds." But before then, in verse 5, God had said, "And it shall be that the rod of the man whom I choose will blossom; thus I will rid Myself of the complaints of the children of Israel, which they make against you."[5] This was why Moses asked the leaders of Israel to bring all their rods, including that of Aaron, and Moses placed the rods before the Lord in the tabernacle.

Notice that on hearing what God said, Moses did not say it was a foolish thing to do. God wanted to finally put an end to the shame in their lives. By the next day, Moses went into the tabernacle and saw that the rod of Aaron had sprouted and blossomed, yielding ripe almonds. God, who made a lifeless rod to bud and become fruitful, is the same God of yesterday, today and forever. In verse 10, "The LORD said to Moses, "Bring Aaron's rod back before the ark of testimony."[6] God wants to showcase your life as a testimony even among unbelievers, and among doubters. But you need to walk in obedience. God said it is a testimony "to be kept as a sign against the rebels, that you may put their complaints away from Me, lest they die."[7]

Time for Change

People may have labeled you by the afflictions that you have been going through but I can assure you that your story is about to change. Fruitfulness is a force. It is a cycle and it's on the inside of you. I pray that you come to the point where you are fruitful whether you like it or not. And I see that power being released on your inside as you read this book. In the Bible, Job says that "There is hope for a tree when it has been cut down."[8] Even if you are disconnected as a branch, there is still hope for you. Yes, there is hope because at the touch of the water of the word of God, you will bud again.

Let me tell you something more: if you want to see a cycle of fruitfulness in your life, be planted by the 'river of living waters'. Stay permanently in the word of God and remain connected to the Lord. To the married woman, God expects you to be fruitful. Don't draw your self-esteem from your husband, but from God. Growing up as young girls and singles, most of us learned about how a man should minister to us. We knew about how he is to love us, bring flowers, open doors and those other things. But in marriage, many are shocked to discover that those fantasies do not always exist. The man too is programmed to have expectations about what a woman should do; to cook in the kitchen and do all those chores that his mother did even though he knew he was marrying a career woman. He gets into the marriage and gets the shockers. We don't take the time to learn how we are to be assets, not liabilities. Draw your self-esteem from God.

Fruits of All Sorts

I love marriage. I love the family. I love the home. God wants us to have happy homes. If you are a fruitful woman, your husband of course will love you. He will have no choice, because you are an asset, not a disgrace or a liability to him. God wants to make a sign out of you. The rod of Aaron budded overnight. It brought forth flowers and fruits that others could partake of. John 15:8 says, "By this My Father is glorified, that you bear much fruit."

Fruit, in this context, means joy, peace, and love. The Bible talks about the fruit of the Spirit. It also talks about the fruits of our lips which is what we say. There are fruits of our hands as well. In Proverbs 31, the virtuous woman gave out the fruits of her hand, and her works caused her to be praised her at the gates of the city. The Bible, of course, talks about the fruits of the womb. It is all-round fruitfulness, and I submit to you that you are like the rod of Aaron. You will bud and bear fruits to put an end to every criticism and complaint against you.

One of the ways to answer your critics is to bear more fruit, and become more successful. Make progress, and keep making progress because the Father will be joyful as you bear more fruit.

The Sarahs of Our Time

I got a call from the United States some time ago from a 45-year-old woman who had just delivered a beautiful baby girl that she had desired for many years. That's the God of fruitfulness. He did it in my life too. And I know that I am a fruitful woman because of the Word of God, that I put in my heart. I see you standing on the Word of God and being fruitful on every side as well.

In Genesis 41:52, Joseph called his second son Ephraim, as he said, "For God has caused me to be fruitful in the land of my affliction."[9] I am sure that you are familiar with the story of Joseph and know about the fact that Jacob, his father, could not move on from Laban's house until Rachel had given birth to Joseph. After she had given birth to Joseph, he went to Laban and told him that it was time for him to go. Based on this principle, you should prayerfully call forth your Joseph. Your Joseph might be a child, the fruit of the womb, or a seed that needs to sprout in your life for you to move to the next level. Joseph said God had caused him to be fruitful even as a slave.[10]

There's fruitfulness as a state of being, and there's fruitfulness as an occurrence. In Genesis 39:1-3, Joseph was a slave in the house of Potiphar, yet he was successful because God was with him. They threw him into prison but his fruitfulness followed him there. If God is with you, wherever you are, you will be fruitful and you will simply stand out. You will shine! So don't complain about your situation. Why was Joseph fruitful? Of course, he was destined to be fruitful. He had been chosen to be fruitful just as you and I have been chosen to bear fruit; and as long as you remain connected to the true Vine, you will always be fruitful and will not run dry. Fruitfulness is a power and a force on your inside. When you have the word of God in you, you are fruitful. Fruitfulness does not occur in isolation; the seed needs to be connected. It is like you have a tree; when its seed falls to the ground, it sprouts and grows into a tree, and begins to bear fruits.

The Vital Connection

You need to be connected to the Lord to bring about fruitfulness. This is where the real connection is, because what you hear from Him is what you act on. This is what brings results. Why was Joseph fruitful? It was because of the covenant of fruitfulness which he carried in him. In Christ, you are a woman or man of covenant, and will be fruitful because you have a covenant with God. If things don't look fruitful right now, do a checkup using what God's word says concerning you in that particular area of need.

For some of us, certain areas of our lives are fruitful and flourishing while some other areas are just dry, and we usually don't like talking about the ugly sides of our lives. We don't want to look at those areas nor want people to talk about them. But those are the areas you should concentrate on. Find the scriptures that speak to those areas of unfruitfulness. When people come to me for counseling, I like to do this. It may be the hard approach, but I ask them: "How long have you been saved?" And if they say ten years, I ask further, "What's your challenge?" After this, I go on to ask the number of scriptures they know that addresses that challenge, with an expectation of at least two. Trusting God for the fruit of the womb? I ask for two scriptures related to that. If you are unable to provide even one, then you have not even begun the journey; because that shows that you do not have God's word inside of you. When we pray using God's word, God makes it happen.

In Jeremiah 1:11, God says to Jeremiah, "What do you see?" He answered, "I see a branch of an almond tree." It may very well have been the same almond tree that Aaron's rod produced, ready to bring forth ripe fruits. God then said to Jeremiah, "Now you are ready and I will hasten My word to perform it."[11] Prophets and ministers simply hasten the word of God that is already inside you, not that in someone else. The word inside of me will produce for me. Likewise, the word in you will produce for you. Do you labor in the word at all? Why was Joseph blessed? He was blessed because he had the word of God in him. God had sworn over his life and this was the same for Abraham. God is not partial. If you are planted in God's word and you abide in His presence, you will inevitably flourish because you are in covenant with God.

There is one other dimension to this. In Genesis 49:22, we see why Joseph was blessed. Jacob, his father, had recognized that Joseph was blessed. He said, "Joseph is a fruitful bough, A fruitful bough by a well; His branches run over the wall."[12] That is the power of prophetic blessing. Prophecy should at all times come from God to His children to give them direction. It hurts leaders and pastors when their members are not flourishing, because the devil would want to make it look like they lacked anointing and power to bless the people. But it is too late for me to be confused about the fact that I am anointed to bless humanity.

Power in the Word

I live by the word of God. In our church, when members share testimonies, my husband and I are excited that the word that was preached from the pulpit is affecting people positively. The Bible says that some hear the word but the word does not mix with faith in their hearts[13], and thus, they remain in a state of unfruitfulness. Some others hear the word, and run with it, and testify to the power in the word. And that's how we know if you have been diligent in the word or not. The prophetic blessing on Joseph was that he was a fruitful branch. By the word of God, Joseph was connected to the Vine forever. Whether in the pit, in Potiphar's house, in prison or wherever else, he was connected and God was with him.

It doesn't matter where you are at the moment. You could be in the valley of the shadow of death, but if God is with you, you will fear no evil. His rod and staff will comfort you. So do not think it strange when you go through the valley because it's all part of the scheme of God to promote you. He wants to make you a testimony. "Joseph was a fruitful bough by the well and branches run over the wall. The archers have bitterly grieved him, shot at him and hated him, but his bough remained in strength."[14] I pray that you 'remain in strength'. His arms were made strong by the hands of the Almighty God of Jacob.

Dreaming Big

You see, the blessing of fruitfulness must be transferred to our children. They must not find it difficult to be fruitful and it must become a normal thing because you pass on the covenant to them.

Even if you are a single woman, dream big. And if you are married, I further emphasize that you dream big. God has put vision in your heart. And let me make an appeal to husbands: give your wives the freedom to realize their potentials. Let them flourish and let them grow. You are her husband by covenant and her destiny is accelerated when you allow her to be everything God has created her to be. Bless your wife and say: "I know that there is seed in you." This is beyond the fruit of the womb. Tell your wife, "I know you can start that business. So, go ahead. I support you." You don't have much choice anyway, because if God has called her, the matter is just as settled.

While still in college, I wondered in prayer to God, "Lord, I have read about some of those great women You have used in ministry. Yet some of them had issues in their marriages…" I wanted to be happily married, and I also knew that God wanted to use me in some way. "Lord," I probed, "How do I reconcile the contradictions?" God assured me that He would give me a husband that would know that I am for God as I am for him. Give your wife the freedom to dream. Don't be threatened. 'Let her go' and let her grow. Of course, this must not get out of hand to the point she leaves you, but even if that happens, God will sort you out. I can assure you that will never happen.

Nobody wants a broken home. Women in particular don't like it. They however like to have the freedom do what God has called them to do. Support your wife. Don't be afraid. She is your crown and beauty. People will envy or appreciate you because of her. She will trace her exploit and victories to God and you. You will share in her glory and joy too. This may not always be convenient, but you need to persevere. Working in partnership with your wife, share in helping out with the kids and other house chores, and don't be verbally abusive in attempts to limit her.

Sometime ago, God gave me a word. "Don't idolize your children," He said to me. Someone had a dream and told me that, "God said you are limiting yourself because of your children. You don't want to go because you're worried about who would take care of the children." I responded, "You're right, Lord." Then, I remembered reading the story of a woman who had the call of God on her life many years ago. In those days, it was strange for women to preach publicly because they would be criticized. She was unwilling to go, because she was caring for her children. Then, things suddenly turned against her. All her children started dying one by one. Yet, it didn't immediately change her attitude towards the call. She wouldn't answer the call until all except one of her kids had died. Then she said, "Yes, Lord, I will do Your will." That saved the life of the last child. She went ahead and God used her powerfully and mightily. Even then, she had a problem with her marriage.

You see, for women, our emotions play a huge role. How do we combine the call of God upon our lives with our marriage? Let me say to you: It is well with you. You are a fruitful woman. Release all the seeds God has put in you, so that when you finally enter heaven, God can say, "Well done, My good and faithful servant."

CHAPTER 6

ROOM
FOR
FRUITFULNESS

I want to start this chapter by saying that the Lord has made room for you, and you will be fruitful in the land He has placed you. This was Isaac's testimony in Genesis 26:22, which says, "For now the LORD has made room for us, and we shall be fruitful in the land." It's important to understand what happened before Isaac got to the point where he could declare this. Discovering this is key to understanding our capacity for fruitfulness.

Some women have had to wait on the Lord for a long time for the fruit of the womb. Some are still waiting. Let me assure you that nothing escapes the power of God. There is room for you. One thing that I like about the power of God is that it always produces a miracle and these are miracles that bring an end to your shame and the intimidations of the devil.

Caging the Devil

Let me show you how to cage the devil. The Bible says in Genesis 26:2, that "The Lord appeared unto Isaac and charged him not to go to Egypt to flee the drought in Gerar, but remain in the land." Isaac sowed in Gerar in obedience to the Lord. Obedience to God is the key to fruitfulness and the weapon that silences the devil. Those who are quick to obey God will be fruitful eventually. They are not ashamed of their so-called image. In most cases, the things God tells you to do may look foolish. Remember, God uses the foolish things of this world to confound the wise. If the devil had known, he would not have crucified the King of Glory. It was through God's foolishness that Jesus went to the cross to die for our sins. The result of that, today, is our fruitfulness.

Isaac obeyed God. There was fruitfulness locked up inside of him. Had he not obeyed God, the fruitfulness that resulted would not have come. God chooses you to be fruitful. In John 15, Jesus in verse 1, said He was the Vine and the Father the Vinedresser. Through that role, God prunes you, if you are a branch connected to the Vine. There will be a time of pruning and temptation. There will be a time of afflictions, but you will be okay if you are connected to Jesus. Fruitfulness does not happen in isolation.

How to Be Connected

You need to be connected to the Holy Ghost and to the people God brings your way. There are people that God will send to help you. It is when you are connected to the Lord in the place of prayer and communion that God will show you the people He is sending to your aid, not by calculations and scheming to get attention.

Jesus said, "If you remain in Me you will bear fruit."[1] This is why I know that God hates barrenness, fruitlessness, and dryness. Jesus does not expect that any branch in Him would be fruitless. Unfruitful branches are cut off. That was what He did with the unfruitful fig tree. He expected fruits from it. The tree had flowers that made it look beautiful on the outside, but it lacked fruits.

Give of Your Substance

One day, I told my husband that I thank God for my official car and that everything was well with us and our church. I then said that I was not going to have any of those possessions on my mind but rather focus on his love and intimacy. Some men are shocked to find out that the most important thing in the mind of a wife, with regard to her relationship, is love and intimacy. Indeed, we women have to be forthright and teach our husbands all of that. Just ensure to use an appealing tone, not make demands as if claiming your right.

A question came up in one of our meetings in the church. "How do I deal with a man that won't release money? He is a miser and is stingy; even when it comes to paying the children's tuition." I I'm frequently asked such questions. And you will agree that when counseling, you have to validate the enquirer first, before agreeing with their own narrative or whatever complaints they might have.

In answering a woman complaining about a stingy husband, I would often say, "Some people are just tight-fisted and stingy by nature, and to open their fist, you need the intervention of God. To such people, it's in their inner being, and perhaps runs in the family. It is possible that the father and mother were stingy and he has been influenced by that." I prefer to respond like that, rather than run down the person. So if your husband or wife is like that, you should pity him or her. This pity should drive you to intercede for that person.

Women, you know, are natural givers. Therefore, if, as a woman, you hold back from giving, you are doing something that is quite abnormal. There are times when I go into my wardrobe and begin to sort out clothes that are still in superb shape but no longer my size, or I have grown tired of them. Then, I give them all out. And because like begets like, my kids are taking a cue from my actions, and are now tremendous givers.

Their acquaintances have started to acknowledge this from school and commend them. You buy beautiful things for them and they say they want to give them out to their friends. They go out to orphanages with me and seeing me give to the needy has rubbed off on them. They don't hesitate to give their precious personal things to needy friends. When you give, you free up space for more blessings from God. When my wardrobe empties out, I begin to look up to God, and He brings more.

Look at it this way. If you keep eating and don't use the washroom, you sure would feel very uncomfortable after a while. Giving relieves us of constipation. These are vital things in life no one else but you can do for yourself. I can't give on your behalf. I can't serve God or man on your behalf. I can't obey God on your behalf. I obey God for myself. I can't breathe for you, as simple as that seems. I can't eat for you. Those are the important things that we do in life.

The Lord made room for Isaac because he obeyed God who had told him not to go to Egypt. What's wrong with going to Egypt? After all, God permitted Abraham to go to Egypt in a similar situation. For Isaac, God specifically said, "Don't go to Egypt. Stay in the land and sow in it. I will be with you and do with you what I said to Abraham."[2]

What has God said to you? If you are sure that God has spoken to you, then do what He said and be persistent. Isaac stayed in Gerar as God commanded him. He had initial troubles with the people of the land, but finally they stopped contending with him; rather, they blessed him. They brought gifts to him and acknowledged that God was with him. In fact, they became afraid of him. The same thing happened to his father, Abraham in Genesis 22. God blessed Abraham on account of his obedience. He made him fruitful and multiplied his possessions.

I believe God will increase and multiply you also. But, don't keep God's blessings to yourself. You need to bless the lives of others. He told Abraham, "In blessing I will bless you and multiply your descendants as the stars of heaven,"[3] because Abraham was willing to offer his only son, Isaac, to God. You must give in order to be fruitful. Except a corn of wheat falls to the ground and dies, Jesus says, it abides alone; but when it dies, it brings forth much fruits.[4]

Giving of your substance may look or feel like dying for a season, but your love and generous heart will rebound to you a hundredfold in due season.

A Sure Promise

The Bible says concerning the fruitfulness of a blessed man, in Psalm 1, that he is planted by the rivers of water, and therefore brings out fruits in his season. Psalm 92 also says that, "Those who are planted in the house of our God shall flourish in the courts of our God." Are you planted where God has put you? Are you walking in obedience? Then, there is no trick of the enemy that would hinder you from being fruitful.

Read the story of Tamar and Judah in Genesis 38. It is not a popular reference with preachers though, because Tamar played the harlot, rather, she pretended to be a harlot. She was married to Judah's first son called Er. His life was cut short because he was a wicked man before God. Generally, Judah's sons were notoriously wicked. Er did not love Tamar, probably because his father was the one that made the arrangements for them to get married. After Er died, the next in line of Judah's sons was Onan. The culture, at that time, was that Tamar would automatically fall to him as a wife. But he did not want her. He proved that by spilling his semen outside of her. Apparently, he was satisfied with sleeping with her but did not want a child from her.

That was cheating because he limited and hindered her. Outwardly, their marriage was fine. She was 'happily married' as they say, but in the privacy of their bedroom, 'nothing was happening.' She was denied what was her legitimate due.

Safe in the Vine

The story of Tamar may be similar to yours. You may have been denied many times what is your due in business, at your work place, or in your matrimonial home. Some people suffer and go through terrible times in the hands of their in-laws. I have news for you, God will deliver you. It all depends on your connection to the Vine. It also depends on what you are doing with what He had told you to do. You need to persevere and maintain a sweet spirit. Do not allow bitterness to ruin the good fruits you are bearing in your life. Yes, you suffer wrong in the home, but don't wear it on your face. Those who resent you will, very soon, return to acknowledge you when they see that God is with you.

There are times, as a Christian when you go through certain things that you can't really explain, but these are signs that some forces are trying to work against you. Yet, you know as a Christian, that no weapon formed against you shall prosper, that every tongue that rises against you in judgment are condemned.[5]

I was in that sort of situation at a time and prayed, "Lord, You told Nicodemus that when one is born again, he or she is like the wind. Make my life like the wind so that nothing evil can grasp me." You must stand with that type of confidence against your enemy. They will think they have caught you, but you will slip through their hands. They will not understand how, and your life would be preserved.

The riotous mob that accused Jesus of blasphemy, because He said He was the Son of God, attempted to push Him down a cliff before the appointed time of His death. No way! He walked through their midst and escaped, leaving them bewildered because He had to die by the Cross as prophesied, not by any other means. They could do Him no harm, until the King of glory was ready to lay down His own life. No one can harm you because you are like the rod of Aaron. God makes a distinction of His children from the riotous mob of sinners who have no covenant with Him.

What happened in the case of Tamar is quite instructive. Onan kept on cheating this woman and breaking the covenant of marriage with her. Eventually Onan, like Er, his late brother, also died suddenly for his wickedness.

After Onan's death, the last born of Judah, Shelah, was not old enough to inherit Tamar to be his wife. She was, therefore, asked to go back to her father's house and remain a widow till the lad was old enough to marry her. When Shelah grew old enough to be married, Judah forgot about Tamar. At this time, the mother of those sons had also died. She must have been a very distraught mother-in-law!

When Tamar heard that her father-in-law was passing by to Timnath "to shear his sheep", she removed her clothes of widowhood and put on something seductive. She veiled her face and went to stay by the wayside to catch Judah's attention. As the man passed by, he thought she was a prostitute. She was not. She had remained pure in her father's house all this while. When she could have given up, she did not because the small boy of six years old, as was their culture, would grow up to marry her. She knew when the boy would become a man, because she was counting the years; but they deliberately did not remember her or what was owed to her.

The story was that Tamar stood there under the guise of a prostitute, and waited for Judah to approach her. Note that she did not approach him but he approached her. "Yes, what would you give me?" She inquired of him, and they reached a deal on a goat, which he promised to send her. In the interim, she demanded a token of surety - his rod and signet ring. The rod had very important connotations with men in those days.

They always carried it wherever they went, and bequeathed it to their sons from generation to generation. She accepted the rod and the signet he was wearing that carried his family name. He gave her all that she asked for, believing that by the next day, he would send the goat to reclaim his rod and signet. So he had sex with her. By the next day, when Judah sent her the payment to reclaim his token, she was nowhere to be found. After months of searching for the 'harlot' without success, Judah forgot the matter; but God did not forget.

Meanwhile, her pregnancy developed large enough to be noticed, and Tamar proved, by her possession of Judah's rod and signet ring the source of her pregnancy. At the end, Judah owned up and said the woman had been more righteous than he. She later delivered twins: Pharez and Zarah.

The Prerogative of God

True, in the New Testament era, all such old practices are done away with. Back at their time, however, Tamar's action was justified because of the injustice she suffered. Right or wrong, Pharez became an ancestor of Jesus Christ. That is the prerogative of God. He is the God of justice. All you need do is obey and serve Him. The mother of Jesus told the servants at the marriage in Cana that whatever the Lord told them to do, they should absolutely obey and do it. Obedience is the secret of fruitfulness.

Tamar had twin boys, all the sons she should have had, at least one apiece from her previous two marriages that had previously denied her the opportunity. The thing really is, you don't need to bother yourself about your enemies or whoever oppresses you, because God who is a righteous judge, sees all the actions of men. When God saw that Leah was hated by her husband, Jacob, He opened her womb but closed, though temporarily, the womb of his preferred wife, Rachel.

Leah sought her husband's favor in vain, but was denied the intimacy every woman cherishes from a husband. Yet God, who instituted marriage, wants us to enjoy all the blessings of marriage, the prosperity, and fruitfulness. Your husband may not be playing his role adequately at the moment, but God will change all that. He will make your husband love you and become more intimate with you, and those things that you desire, God will bring your way. You must, however, first turn to the God of fruitfulness. Do not curse your husband. No, just love him.

For the men reading this, whose wives are yet to bear them any children, I charge you never to curse your wife, no matter what. Love her as a part of you. Turn to the God of fruitfulness and He will make you fruitful. Leah had sons after sons while hoping her husband would consider them and turn in her direction. She wanted Jacob's heart but Rachel, her sister, got all the attention of their husband and that was her own affliction. In the meantime, God prospered other areas of her life. Your business may be prospering while the main longing of your soul is the fruit of the womb. Wait, God is going to come through for you. While you wait, continue to thank God for that area of your life that is blooming.

At the end of the day, Rachel died and was buried as Jacob returned to his homeland. She died in labor while in labor with her second child. Leah lived on with her husband, Jacob. Rachel had Jacob's love but for a short time. She had two children: Joseph and Benjamin. It is probable that she died because she went out of covenant with God. She stole the idol of her father, Laban, when the family was relocating to Canaan. Of course, God could not have been happy with that. That means her heart was not totally with the God of Jacob, her husband. She sat on the idol when her father searched for it, claiming she was menstruating and should not rise up. She died in labor probably because her father placed a curse on whoever took his idol. It did not have to happen to her, but at the end of the day, Leah had Jacob fully to herself. And when she reached full age and died, Leah was buried next to her husband, Jacob. They were together in death.

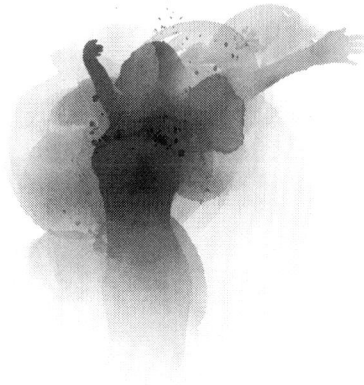

CHAPTER 7

HER
OWN
BUSINESS

The word entrepreneur is from the word enterprise, which, according to the Oxford *Advanced Dictionary*, means any project or undertaking, especially one that is difficult, or needs courage to undertake. We need courage to do a whole lot of things. The virtuous woman, in Proverbs 31:10 -31, is a good example of a courageous woman. She exemplifies courage and we do have a lot to learn from her.

Woman, You Need Courage

You need courage to start a business, a building project, or to move forward in your career; or even to go to school and get an education.

When we were younger, some of us did not have the opportunity to go to a school. But, I know of some women that, after having had children, decided to go back and get a formal education. Indeed, it takes courage to do this.

It takes a lot of courage to get married and start a family, because in this day and age, we see and hear all manner of evils afflicting homes that result in broken marriages. Some young ladies, out of fear, decide in their hearts not to marry or raise a family. Some marry but do so halfheartedly.

You also need courage to carry out the responsibilities the Lord has given to you, especially as a woman. This is because women are always loaded with responsibilities in the home, and the society expects so much from us because God has ordained us as life-givers. That's what Eve, the name of the first woman means, a life-giver. Every woman should see herself from this perspective. Whether you are single or married, whatever your age, understand that you are a life-giver because that is what God has ordained us to be.

The tough question now is: How does the woman cope as a life-giver, with so much responsibility with parents to care for, children to nurture, a husband to please, help and support; a career to attend to and a business to grow? Yet, all of these are to flourish simultaneously in our hands. Women surely needs courage!

Woman, You Need God

God would have you know that you cannot go at it alone. As women, we need His help and strength. He gives strength to the weak. He is the one that encourages, enables and gives favor to His needy daughters. He blesses and is always available to help us if we depend on Him. We need to realize that there is no way, in our own strength or ability, that we can successfully accomplish all the various tasks we are encumbered with.

Let's see the woman's responsibilities from the angle of an entrepreneur, having the understanding that an enterprise is any project that needs courage and might be difficult to accomplish. We need to have the mentality of an entrepreneur towards all of our responsibilities, not only towards our businesses, but even towards our families.

Enriching the Family

From Proverbs 31:27, we learn that the virtuous woman "watches over the ways of her household, and does not eat the bread of idleness." She guards her family, is watchful, and makes sure that she makes a profit - not necessarily monetary - for the family. The family is a place wherein you endeavor to invest your whole life into others, your children in particular, so they can grow up to positively influence their generation. It's therefore not only about financial reward when it comes to raising a family, but a reward that is eternal and would affect the nation and other nations too.

God ordained children to be born through families, through wholesome marriages; marriages where there is love and stability. This is why my husband and I advise that you enter and maintain your marriage with open and watchful eyes. You must make the best of it because you will give account of your privileges in marriage. Children must be raised in the right atmosphere. This is so crucial to their destiny. They need an atmosphere that blesses and encourages them. You can see that God has called women to influence lives on His behalf.

God said, "Be fruitful, multiply, have dominion, subdue the earth and take possession."[1] In short, God is saying, take your place as a woman. We have come a long way since the Stone Age. Things have improved considerably. All kinds of things are being manufactured from business to business, and this is what God expects from us because He has ordained progress for the earth. He wants to impact the earth through you and me.

The call is to have courage to take the place God has ordained for us. Take the family God has given you as a business. Watch over it; make good use of it. You may not necessarily hold the microphone and stand before many people to preach and teach, but what you impart through your household, can equally have impact on multitudes of people for eternity. Your task of raising that child or children is a major business that can bless countless people and make a difference in your environment and even in your nation.

Some women do not like to be told to start something new, especially when they have not seen anyone do it in their part of the world. They are afraid. But, you should courageously start whatever God lays in your heart, because of what He wants to do through it. God plans to influence lives through you and change this world. He wants to make a difference in the world through you.

The virtuous woman, in Proverbs 31, accepted life from various levels. She accepted life first, as a wife, but before that, she accepted life as a single woman since she wasn't born a wife. Describing the virtuous woman while single, verse 10 states, "Who can find a virtuous wife? For her worth is far above rubies." This means that even before she got married, she had begun to prepare herself with noble character. She was not a peddler of gossip nor did she backbite against others. She watched over her own life, because she knew that, eventually, she would have to watch over the lives of others.

The Priceless Worth of a Woman

The Bible says in Proverbs 18:22, that he that finds a wife finds a good thing and obtains favor of the Lord. Woman, see yourself as an asset, even while still single, to a future godly man who God has prepared and needs a suitable help mate. He needs someone who would bless his life, a giver, a woman of noble character. The Bible says, when such a man finds his mate, he has obtained favor because the woman is favor personified. That is our first name, "favor".

The intention of God is that the woman should carry so much favor and joy with her, to bless anyone who comes in contact with her. The impact of a woman is contagious. We impact lives. Even as a single woman, prepare yourself to impact lives. You may not have been born in a very stable marriage or a cozy environment, but since you now have realized that you are accountable for other lives, you need to prepare yourself. By the time a woman becomes a wife, her worth has gone far more than rubies. How? You see, money doesn't buy virtue.

The virtuous woman is the portrait of *The Real Woman* the Bible exults. Her husband has full confidence in her. He can trust her, so that he seeks none else. He wouldn't have to look left or right. He has no need of 'spoil'. He has no need of 'game'; he lacks nothing of value because he has a virtuous woman by his side. She will do him good and not evil.

Do Not Hurt

Some women are tempted to hurt their husbands. They want to revenge his ill treatment because, sometimes, men tend to be unfair. Just imagine a husband that does not treat his wife fairly and cheats on her. Yet, you see, the Bible says that God is the defender of the weak, and that is why we have to learn and rely on Him. I tell you, "He is a rewarder of those who diligently seek Him."[2] But, we must do our own part. Our role as blessings to our husbands, is not dependent on the man. The Bible did not say to do him good when he's good to you. It says do him good all the days of your life. Your purpose in life is to do your husband good; then you watch how God will, in return, reward you. Decide in your heart to be a blessing to your man, even if you feel he does not deserve it, and see how God will reward you. God knows how best to do these things. Blessing your husband will result in you receiving healing, because you might be hurting. Men might have abused you. Your own husband might have abused you too. Jesus wants you to know that He is by your side.

Jesus, Our Savior

In John 8, there was a woman caught in adultery and in those days, whoever was caught in adultery was stoned to death. That was under the law before Jesus came. This woman was caught, as the men said, "in the very act". The men gathered to mete out her instant judgment by stoning her. They probably saw a flash of opportunity to rope in Jesus too, so they might accuse Him of something worthy of death. So, they brought her to Jesus with iron-cast accusations: "She was caught in the very act of adultery. Moses' law condemns her to instant death. But what do you say?" They asked Jesus.

Accused of sin publicly by such a mob of religious bigots, the woman was speechless. She was guilty. But bringing the guilty to the Savior and expecting Him to condemn the offender, who is in need of salvation, exposes the ignorance of the Scribes and Pharisees. They did not appreciate the fact that Jesus came to save the lost and give life.[3] Any wonder, most of them did not take the advantage of Jesus' offer of salvation. They said that the woman was caught in the very act but interestingly, they did not pull the man along to be condemned too. They let him go scot-free because, as people say, "it's a man's world." That is very common today. Many men have a tendency to cheat, supplant and oppress women. This incident and Jesus' response to them, offers the hurting woman a lot of hope.

Here is another scenario. You are due for promotion in the office and know it's your entitlement, but your male boss just wouldn't give you, preferring a male colleague who probably isn't working half as hard as you and joined the firm after you. But never mind, because Jesus is with you to lift you up. He is the defender of the oppressed.

If you are oppressed as a woman, take courage and rest in the Lord. Allow Him to fight for you. He will do it, and do it well. Don't try to take laws into your own hands and try to fight it out on your abilities and strength. That is most likely to fail. God wants us to depend on Him.

Rather than condemn the woman as the mob wanted, Jesus forgave her sins and let her go free to sin no more. Jesus would not condemn any penitent sinner who is willing to forsake sinful practices. Sin is a destroyer. Let us settle that right now in our minds. When sin is rampant in a person's life, it eventually destroys him or her. Only Jesus sets one free from sin. His shed blood on the cross washes away all sins.

Use What You Have

Back to the businesswoman in Proverbs 31, she rules and in fact, works with eager hands. She's like a merchant ship bringing her food from afar. She gets up while it is yet dark and provides food for her family. She doesn't go after her career to get money and forget about her family, leaving them at the mercy of whomever. No, she has a business approach to her family. She makes sure she does her shopping with extra care and her family is well catered for. Even if she needed to be away for a while, she makes sure everything is in place for the family, and that they do not they lack anything. Yes, she has her business but the family does not feel like she loves her business more than her family. This is *The Real Woman*.

The virtuous woman considers a field and buys it, and out of her earnings she plants a vineyard. She is financially empowered. God wants women to be financially empowered. The Bible speaks of some women who followed Jesus. They were women of substance, who ministered to Him out of their own resources. Joanna, the wife of Herod's steward and some other women were mentioned by name.

The woman's financial empowerment is not to show off or try to prove that she is better than the man, or try to show she has more money than her husband. It is not about hidden agendas either, as some women are known to do, of buying a land in your name or building a house secretly and not letting your husband know about it.

The real woman is humble. God wants to empower you financially, but He is interested in both your attitude and what you do with your finances. If we will use our resources to build lives, the environment and nation; if we would finance the gospel, then God will put large chunk of funds in our hands. That is why He wants us to take courage and start a business, whatever the business that is laid on your heart may be. It could be baking cakes, fashion designing, whatever else it is, even if you've not seen anybody do it. Be a first, a pioneer in your business area. That is what God wants to make out of you.

Bless the World

The virtuous woman affected the lives of others. Verse 20 says, "She extends her hand to the poor, yes, she reaches out her hands to the needy." As women, we are mothers even if you are yet to give birth to your own children. We are naturally mothers at heart, and that is what God expects of us. We are to bless other lives and help the less privileged in the society. God wants us to be charity minded. The Bible accounts of the generosity of Dorcas in Acts 9. She was full of charitable works and good deeds. When she suddenly took ill and died, all the widows around her lamented her passing so much that God was touched. He called in Peter to raise her up. She came back to life because of the cries of those whom she had helped. That should be our testimony. When we die, we should be missed.

Therefore, take responsibilities and be relevant. It's not to show off any kind gesture we have done; it's about being relevant wherever you are in that little corner of your city. Make sure you are affecting one life or the other. There would be tremendous reward for your deeds. God expects noble things from us. That is a foregone conclusion, and that is why it aches my heart to see prostitutes on our streets. Their immoral trade is not noble at all. Women are not to propagate sexual diseases of any sort through any form of immorality. We must be known for nobility, not for evil things; not for peddling gossips or backbiting.

Be On Your Guard

The sixth verse of 2 Timothy 3 talks about evil people who find their way into the homes and lives of gullible women. We must not be gullible and weak willed. Eve failed in the beginning on that score. God has empowered us in Christ. We will not make the same mistake and fall into deceit. Deceit is the weapon of the enemy, and it's what the devil has been using against many women. He tells you to cheat your boss in your organization. If you do that, you are not likely to rise in your career. Your boss may not see what you do, but God sees everything. In your business, if you are not faithful or accountable, then it isn't likely to grow; and God wants your business to grow. He said we should have nothing to do with anything that is ungodly. We should not sit down with gossipers and backbiters.

Proverbs 14:1 says, "The wise woman builds her house, But the foolish pulls it down with her hands." We are home builders. We are life builders. We have to watch how we spend our time and guard our lives and be careful of who we move around with. We must affect the lives of others positively. The women who failed in the past are not our pattern. They were weak-willed. God gives us strength where we are weak. We will not be deceived anymore. It is deception when a woman feels that when she sleeps with men, she can make money. There are noble ways of making money. Such things should not be found with us so that the nation would be proud of the women.

Let's take our place and build our nations in our own small ways. God had placed us in various places, fields, businesses and careers so that we might influence what goes on there and make a difference. If this whole world was full of men, it would be a very boring place.

That's why God brought in women for variety, to spice up the atmosphere and cause things to move forward. God wants us to take courage in that and build our families. You might say, "Lord, I want to build a family, but I haven't gotten a husband yet." God is faithful. He has said you should work on yourself and make yourself an asset, then the good man He has for you will find you.

CHAPTER 8

THE PURPOSE-DRIVEN WOMAN

Let's now focus on the purpose driven woman. The issues here are so deep and loaded that we must pay close attention. Romans 8:28 tells us, "And we know that all things work together for good to those who love God, to those who are the called according to His purpose."

Christians often quote this scripture, but many are prone to leaving out most of its juice. For instance, we try to encourage others when we say, "Don't worry, all things work together for good." And I quite agree that all things do work together for good but this is where many stop. There is no point in encouraging a friend who is going through a hard time by saying that he or she should not worry, that all things will work together for their good. Some even go a step further to saying that all things work together for good to those who love God. The full verse says, "All things work together for good to those who love God, to those who are the called according to His purpose."[1]

Do you know that there are so many people walking aimlessly on the streets of our cities, without any purpose in life? Sure, they think they have a purpose, but they just loiter around. Nothing is driving them nor are they driving anything. They lay about, chasing the wind, going to and fro and being tossed about by every circumstance and situation. The Bible says, even for those who are believers, that we should not be tossed to and fro by every wind of doctrine.[2] People are not just being tossed about by every wind of doctrine; they are being tossed to and fro by every situation.

A Purposeful Lifestyle

There are three categories of people. First, there are those who are not driven by a purpose. They are weakly driven, poverty driven, and society driven. They remain in a poor state of mediocrity, controlled by external forces and tossed to and fro with no purpose in life. Amazingly, God did not make anything or anyone without a purpose. Ecclesiastes 3:1 says, "To everything there is a season, a time for every purpose under heaven."

But when the purpose of anything is not known, abuse is inevitable. If I do not know that the purpose of the microphone is to amplify my voice, I would most likely use it for something else. It could become a toy for my children to play with. The drummer looking for his drum sticks might pick up whatever he finds on the floor to beat his drums. But that is abuse. And one of the reasons why a lot of women are being abused is because they don't even know their purpose in life; so they allow themselves to be abused. When you know your purpose, you don't allow anyone to abuse you.

Second, there is a category of people who unconsciously become purpose driven. They don't know how; but find themselves doing the right things, and think it's a hobby. They are purpose driven, but are not conscious of it. They are working with their purpose to some extent, but are not aware of it. To such, even what God wants them to do becomes a hobby. They do the right things, but halfheartedly; since, to them, it's not the main thing in their life. Yet, that thing gives them so much joy because it's something they do effortlessly. Just because the task doesn't look mainstream, they disregard it at will.

You find this attitude common with those who are engaged in what they regard as minor jobs. For example, someone might consider being a baker a minor job compared to working in a bank. Agreed, those are two different fields, but that does not make one less important to the other. Imagine being called to beautify women and prepare brides for their wedding day, and you know you should open a saloon; but because you feel that you deserve more, given your academic qualifications, you look down on that calling. To the glory of God and with all humility, I have a master's degree in architecture, but what I am doing is completely different. I thank God for the greater call to build the lives of people rather than to build skyscrapers even though that can bring in loads of money, but can't save a life. I have many friends that are still architects, but that is because God wants them to be there. Just be conscious about your own purpose.

Third, there are those who are deliberately purpose driven. They know their purpose in life; have come to know it and this is their driving force and motivation behind everything they do. They have accepted their purpose or purposes and are moving on with it. They are excelling in it.

How to Be Purpose-Driven

You may want to know how to be purpose-driven. The text in Romans says, "All things work together for good to those who love God."[3] Yes, you may love God and you are definitely called according to His purpose. The question however is, are you working in the reality of that purpose?

You need to understand what God has called you to do. What He called you for is what He expects to get out of you, because God is an investor. He didn't just make us for the fun of it. You are made for a purpose. God allowed you to be born into this earth because He wants to get some glory out of you. The Bible says we are made for His good pleasure, to give Him pleasure, and to glorify Him.[4] But you see, we can only give God pleasure when we stay in His presence, not just in the church but also in our homes, because the Bible says that God is looking for those who will worship Him in spirit and in truth.[5] He has purposed some areas of life where you will be planted and where you will make an impact for Him.

It's not enough, therefore, that we worship God all day long in church; there are people out there that we must contact and impact to join in the worship of God. Whatever it is that you are doing, do it with a difference, because God has ordained for you to do it well.

What Is Purpose?

The simple definition of purpose is the intention of a thing or the aim or function of it. Do you want your life to count? Then, have purpose in whatever you do. Be motivated. Let whatever you do have meaning and of value to God. What did God have in mind for you when He made you? The place of purpose is the place of fulfillment; it's the place of blossoming. It is not a place of complacency. The feeling of 'having arrived' means you have finished your work and are ready to die. You cease to be relevant on earth.

To move into this place of purpose, first ask yourself, 'Who am I?' Be very real with yourself. Get a sheet of paper and begin to write the answers that come to your mind. Even if you think you are already walking in your purpose, ask yourself the question all the same, because you may not be in the center of what God wants you to do. Let me give your some images to think about. See yourself as a seed that is planted and then begins to grow. It dies but the cell revives and begins to grow. The Bible says, "Except a corn of wheat falls to the ground and dies, it abides alone."[6]

Yes, sometimes, you go through situations that makes you look like you are dead. Some of the things we do have to die for our real purpose to come out. You need to die to yourself. Jesus had to die physically on the cross before His purpose of saving humanity was realized. That's the way He was able to multiply Himself in our lives as Christians. It's the same with the seed that is planted; it first must die, then come alive and grow. Next, the leaves shoot out and it begins to bear fruits.

Don't Stop

When the seed says I am a seed, or I am a leaf, is that all God desires from it? It has not gotten to her final usefulness yet. So don't box yourself in yet. Keep asking God, 'I know I am in purpose now, but what is it for this year? You said you will show me the path of life, for in Your presence there is fullness of joy. Am I still on track?'

It is when God shows you the path of life and you are walking in it, that you enjoy the fullness of joy; not only when we sing praises and worship God in church. It is possible to praise and worship God in church but experience gloom at home when one is not in the place of purpose. When you ask to know who you are, you don't just say, "I am Nike." That is just a name. Who is the real you? You might say, "I am funny, humorous, a people-friendly person." That is, you look at your qualities, at what is on your inside. Go further and ask, "Why was I born or why was I created?" You were not created because your parents wanted to have a child. For some of us, our parents didn't plan to have us; we just popped up unannounced. Others don't even know their parents.

Every Human in the Eye of God

Sometime ago, at the Real Woman Foundation where we try to rehabilitate displaced young girls, especially girls who have gotten pregnant or those with young babies but have no place they call a home, we had a naming ceremony for a new baby girl. I was so thrilled because its young mother had been a prostitute, but had taken on a new turn, having given her life to Jesus Christ right there in the brothel where we picked her up about two and half months earlier. She had watched a documentary on Real Women Foundation, which touched her heart and caused her to give her life to Christ. She does not know the father of her baby because she got pregnant while in prostitution. For that child, it wasn't because her parents wanted her to be born that she was born. Do you get the picture?

The young mother began to see God's hand as we prayed over her baby. We dedicated her to the Lord and surnamed her Emmanuel after Christ, because the young lady, like I said, didn't know who the father of her baby was, nor does she want the girl to bear her own last name. That baby has a purpose, even though she was conceived in sin. God has a plan for her for allowing her to be born. She could have died in the womb. There was another lady with a similar situation who was trying to abort when someone came to tell us about it. She tried to abort the fetus, but the child refused to die. Later the child was born, a beautiful baby, with a purpose in life. To God be all the glory!

So when you ask what your purpose is in life, you do not go to your parents. You go to God who allowed conception to take place. He's the One who has something in His mind for you. Before I was formed in my mother's womb He knew me. The word of God is your first stop in finding what your purpose is in life. And then you look at your potentials. What could I be that I am not? And that is an interesting question. What are the untapped abilities in me?

Another way you can discover your purpose is by asking God specific questions about yourself. If you do, He will answer you. He promised in Jeremiah 33:3, "Call to Me, and I will answer you, and show you great and mighty things, which you do not know." God wants to show us things. It's just that many of us have not called upon Him.

Remember in John 3, Nicodemus went to Jesus because he was astounded by the miracles Jesus was performing, and said "Rabbi, we know that You are a teacher come from God; for no one can do these signs that You do unless God is with him." Jesus answered and said to him, "Most assuredly, I say to you, unless one is born again, he cannot see the kingdom of God." Jesus was focusing on the 'person' while Nicodemus, in the subsequent discourse, was concerned about 'the day' or event of natural birth. So who are you?

What is it that God has made you to be? That is where to start. The difference between you and I is who I am on the inside, different from whom you are on your inside. So it's a matter of who I am, who God has said I am. This will enable me to do what God has ordained for me, and with that, impact my generation the way God wants me to.

The Christian's Primary Purpose in Life

God has given us a commission to preach the word. That's in Mark 16 and Matthew 28. He said we should preach the gospel to all the creatures in all nations. The scripture says, "Go therefore and make disciples of all the nations, baptizing them in the name of the Father and of the Son and of the Holy Spirit, teaching them to observe all things that I have commanded you; and lo, I am with you always, even to the end of the age."[7] Amen.

So how do you evangelize and win souls for Christ? You do that when you are purposeful. Whatever God has called you to do will definitely impact other people. No matter what, your light will shine, and God will get all the glory. Even if you work as a beauty consultant for a wedding, for example, you prepare the bride for her wedding day. You make her look beautiful on the outside, but I challenge you to let her be impacted by your lifestyle also, for the glory of God.

Some will come back when they run into problems, because they have found out that it's not just about having beautiful looks on the outside on a wedding day, you have told them that after every wedding, there is a marriage. Or you have counseled them to let their hair remain beautiful for their husbands all through marriage. We can impact our world in so many ways. Are you called to be a mother of children? Do it with all the grace and potentials inside of you.

God's Building

When I began to reach out to young girls who were hurting, I looked back and I found out that indeed, my primary gift was compassion. Whatever the case may be, you can't run away from your purpose, because the Bible says, "It is the purpose of God that will stand."[8] Isaiah 40:8 says, "The grass withers, the flower fades, But the word of our God stands forever." The word that God has given you will stand.

Jesus said to Peter in Matthew 16:18, "…on this rock [or revelation] I will build My church, and the gates of Hades shall not prevail against it." The Church represents the 'called out' ones, or the *ecclesia* of God. The Church, therefore is not the building. It's the people. Upon this revelation, I will build my people and the gates of hell will not be able to control them or overcome them. Upon this rock of revelation, that is upon what He has said to me, God will build my life and the enemy cannot prevail against me. Satan cannot prevail against you when you are in the purpose of God. When you are walking in the light of God's revelation for you, you will not be defeated. Circumstances and situations will change, but the very purpose of God in your life will stand.

It is when you begin to release the gifts and potentials, abilities and the things you love doing, that you begin to enjoy real peace; peace like never before, peace like a river. And you know what, God is interested in us walking in the light of our purposes, because He is looking for fruits of various kinds - not just the fruit of the womb - from our lives. Yes, He is interested in the fruits of the womb because He wants us to give Him godly offspring. Beyond that, God wants profit for His investments in us.

Will He derive glory from the things you are doing? God is eager. He is anxious for you to reveal Him. That's why He would allow His children to be in whatever and every kind of field. He has different assignments for all of us. Don't say you are the light of the church or the salt of the church. He wants you to be the salt of the earth. You are the light of the world, not the light of the word. The word of God gives us light to reach the world. All of us cannot be within the four walls of the church building. Many of us should be out there where we can impact the lives of so many people.

I don't have any problems with women who preach in church. Preach everywhere you are. When I sensed that God had called me, and as I began to give attention to it in some way, some people raised the question if it was right for women to preach in church.

My reply has always been, I don't have anything to say about that, because I have not limited myself to the four walls of the church. I tell myself, my husband can keep the four walls of the church, I will take every other place that is outside the four walls including the buses, the club houses, the beer parlors; those places people go and would not come to church. So where do you have the problem? If prejudice would not let you preach in church, as a woman, go wherever else and preach Jesus.

A Step Higher Than Marriage

When I got married, I thought that my purpose was to be as close as I could be to my husband. And there is nothing wrong with that, and God wants us to be close to our husbands. The problem was that I thought that was my only life's purpose. However, every time I tried to achieve what I had in mind, I failed. I couldn't achieve it in the way I wanted to achieve it. There was just this emptiness that I sensed inside of me, because I kept feeling we were not close enough. He was pastor in another church at the time. Then a few years later, when I joined him full time in ministry, I thought that working together in the church office would make us really close. If that's not God's ultimate purpose for my life, what else could it be? How naïve I was then!

It was therefore a great discovery for me when God opened my eyes to see that I could be used of God in the area of using the compassion in me for those who are trusting God for the fruit of the womb. I also had to trust God for the fruit of the womb. I don't like to say how long I waited because it is very short compared to what others have gone through. For me, it was a short time. But during that time, I didn't consider it short. Every month I knew what it was like to expect to be pregnant and then you see your period and you become discouraged. It felt like I was failing. I have news for all waiting mothers, you are not failing and you have not failed. You are only waiting on God. The time of God has not just come for you to have your baby but it will happen.

Come to think of it, we all wait for God for one thing or another. Mine may be the fruit of the womb; yours may be for your business to grow. You may be waiting on God for reconciliation between you and your father or your mother. You may be waiting on God for the success of an exam that you have repeated again and again.

While waiting to be pregnant, I would sometimes become so discouraged, but my husband wouldn't be bothered. And that used to leave me so frustrated that it often drove us apart. When we came together to pray, he wouldn't even mention our 'desperate' need for children in his prayers; the height of my frustration would reach the heavens! There was one such day, after we had prayed together, that he realized I was angry. He noticed my mood and asked, "What is it? Why are you not happy? We have just finished praying, and you should be happy." Of course, I wasn't happy because he did not mention that area when he prayed. In my own opinion, he was not interested in that area… bla bla bla! No, my waiting time was not long, but it was long enough to make me understand the feelings of a waiting mother.

When you are purpose driven, you will not settle for less. You think in terms of your potential. What is it that I am supposed to be that I have not been? You are always probing your mind for more discoveries. And when you find one, you go for it. A purpose driven woman will give it all her potential. Check out the Proverbs 31 woman. I think that's about the most marked place in my Bible. She released all her potentials. You can see that she was purposeful. She was useful to her family and community. She made impact. Her life counted for good. At the end of the day, her husband could rise and call her blessed. Her children also, even her works spoke for her.

As a woman, I want you to know that God has ordained you to be fruitful. This is not just about the fruit of the womb. He has put seeds inside you in line with your purpose in life. Your fruits will speak for you. Your fruits will abide in whatever work you are involved in. You might be called to be a career woman, a banker or whatever; there will be fruits. Years down the line, there will be people that would trace their greatness or their successes to you.

BOOK ENDNOTES

Chapter 1

1 - Job 28:1
2 - Genesis 2:22
3 - 2 Samuel 6:20
4 - Luke 19:13

Chapter 2

1 - Hebrews 6:10
2 - Esther 2
3 - Genesis 41:51
4 - 1 Timothy 4:14
5 - 1 Chronicles 21:13
6 - Genesis 29:31
7 - Esther 2:4
8 - Proverbs 16:7
9 - 1 Corinthians 9:16
10 - 1 Corinthians 9:5

Chapter 3

1 - Psalm 30:5
2 - Genesis 2:23
3 - Isaiah 43:19
4 - Isaiah 42:9
5 - Ruth 1:18
6 - Isaiah 46:9
7 - Isaiah 41:10
8 - John 14:18
9 - Genesis 3:15
10 - Revelation 12:13
11 - Ecclesiastes 7:8
12 - Ephesians 1:18
13 - Matthew 6:21

Chapter 4

1 - Jeremiah 1:5
2 - Psalm 30:5
3 - Psalm 30:7
4 - Psalm 127:4
5 - Jeremiah 1:12

Chapter 5

1 - John 15:16

2 - John 15:1
3 - 2 Corinthians 12:9
4 - Exodus 16:1-3
5 - Numbers 17:5
6 - Numbers 17:10
7 - Numbers 17:10
8 - Job 14:7
9 - Genesis 41:52
10 - Genesis 41:1-42:2
11 - Jeremiah 1:12
12 - Genesis 49:22
13 - Hebrews 4:2
14 - Genesis 49:23

Chapter 6
───────────

1 - John 15:4
2 - Genesis 26:2
3 - Genesis 22:17
4 - John 12:24
5 - Isaiah 54:17

Chapter 7
───────────

1 - Genesis 1:28
2 - Hebrews 11:6
3 - Luke 19:10

Chapter 8
───────────

1 - Romans 8:28
2 - Ephesians 4:14
3 - Romans 8:28
4 - Ephesians 2:10
5 - John 4:23
6 - John 12:2
7 - Matthew 28:19
8 - Proverbs 19:21

NIKE ADEYEMI

Nike Adeyemi is an international speaker and a global voice of love to nations. She teaches and demonstrates God's love to individuals and communities.

She is the president of Real Woman International Inc. and the founder of The Real Woman Foundation through which many young women have been sheltered, healed and empowered to live amazing lives.

At her Love Home Orphanage, many children thrive, assured of a bright future. On her global TV broadcast, Real Woman with Nike Adeyemi, she shares wisdom on various life issues. She has authored several books.

Nike is an avid learner, despite her masters degrees in Architecture and Business Administration, she further trained in Strategic Perspectives for Non-Profit Management and other leadership courses as she pursues her dream of building lives, to see many more whole and living their dreams too.

Married to her sweetheart Sam, and blessed with three amazing children, she has nurtured and trained many more at Daystar Christian Center and around the world.

For more, visit **nikeadeyemi.com**.

FOR THIS BOOK AND OTHER TITLES
BY NIKE ADEYEMI,
VISIT WWW.AMAZON.COM

24175446R00067

Made in the USA
Columbia, SC
19 August 2018